ENCYCLOPEDIA OF GOOD HEALTH

HUMAN SEXUALITY

ENCYCLOPEDIA OF GOOD HEALTH

HUMAN SEXUALITY

Series Editors

MARIO ORLANDI, Ph.D., M.P.H.

and

DONALD PRUE, Ph.D.

Text by

ANNETTE SPENCE

Facts On File Publications
New York • Oxford

A FRIEDMAN GROUP BOOK

First published in 1989 by Facts On File Publications, Inc.
460 Park Avenue South
New York, New York 10016

Library of Congress Cataloging-in-Publication Data

Spence, Annette.
Human sexuality.

(Encyclopedia of good health)
Includes index.
1. Sex instruction for youth. I. Title. II. Series.
HD35.S625   1988   613.9′5′088055   87-20122
ISBN 0-8160-1666-6

British CIP data available upon request

ENCYCLOPEDIA OF GOOD HEALTH: HUMAN SEXUALITY
was prepared and produced by
Michael Friedman Publishing Group, Inc.
15 West 26th Street
New York, New York 10010

Designer: Rod Gonzalez
Art Director: Mary Moriarty
Illustrations: Kenneth Spengler

Typeset by BPE Graphics, Inc.
Color separated, printed, and bound in Hong Kong by South Seas
International Press Company Ltd.

1 3 5 7 9 10 8 6 4 2

About the Series Editors

Mario Orlandi is chief of the Division of Health Promotion Research of the American Health Foundation. He has a Ph.D. in psychology with further study in health promotion. He has written and edited numerous books and articles, among them The American Health Foundation Guide to Lifespan Health *(Dodd Mead, 1984), and has received numerous grants, awards, and commendations. Orlandi lives in New York City.*

Dr. Donald M. Prue is a management consultant specializing in productivity improvement and wellness programs in business and industrial settings. He was formerly a senior scientist at the American Health Foundation and holds a doctorate in clinical psychology. He has published over forty articles and books on health promotion and was recognized in the Congressional Record *for his work. Prue lives in Houston, Texas.*

About the Author

Annette Spence received a degree in journalism from the University of Tennessee at Knoxville. Her articles have appeared in Redbook, Weight Watchers Magazine, Cosmopolitan, *and* Bride's, *and she has contributed to a number of books. Spence is associate editor for Whittle Communications, a health media company in New York City. She lives in Stamford, Connecticut.*

C O N T

E N T S

How to Use
This Book

Human Sexuality is part of a six-volume encyclopedia series of books on health topics significant to junior-high students. These health topics are closely related to each other, and, for this reason, you'll see references to the other volumes in the series appearing throughout the book. You'll also see references to the other pages *within* this book. These references are important because they tell you where you can find more interrelated and interesting information on the specific subject at hand.

Like each of the books in the series, this book is divided into two sections. The first section tells you why it's a good idea for you to know about this health topic and how it affects you. The second section helps you find ways to improve and maintain your health. We include quizzes and plans designed to help you see how these health issues are related to you. It's your responsibility to take advantage of them and apply them to your life. Even though this book was written expressly for you and other people your age, you are the one who's in control of learning from it and exercising good health habits for the rest of your life.

P A R T I :

What's Important For Me To Know About Sexuality?

It might be better to start this book by asking "What *isn't* important for me to know about sex and hormonal changes?" The truth is there's no time like the present for you to learn all you can about this health topic. As a teenager, you're just beginning to experience a whirlwind of physical, emotional, and social changes, and by understanding what these changes are and why they're happening, you'll be better able to appreciate them. Plus, the more you understand yourself, the better equipped you will be to handle these sometimes trying times. After all, growing up isn't easy. Not only do you have your changing body to deal with, you're also confronting feelings you have never noticed before—new, often confusing attitudes about friends, family, and yourself, and responsibilities that seem larger than life.

Frankly, many of the things you're going through now have to do with sex. For all the mystery, hype, and problems associated with sex, it's actually a fundamental life function. It's going to be an interesting and important part of your life from now on. On the next pages you'll see how your body is readying you for adulthood, and, once you get there, what sex is all about.

Your Body Is Changing by Leaps and Bounds!

It might start in the shower; you'll suddenly notice new hairs around your genitals. If you're a girl, you'll notice little bumps on your chest where your breasts will someday be. If you're a boy, your genitals will begin to grow at a faster rate. Once you notice one little change, you'll feel that in the time it takes to turn around twice, something else has happened. Perhaps hair will begin growing under your arms or you'll get a pimple for the first time. In a matter of a few years, your body will transform from a child's to an adult's. At times you'll find these changes exciting. At other times, this transition may cause you embarrassment.

You're witnessing an incredible interplay of body chemicals within you, called hormones, that stimulate all these changes. You'll often hear this period called puberty. Don't rush it. Once you're totally grown up, there's no going back. It's as much fun to be an adult as it is to be a teenager, but every phase of life is very different. For now, concentrate on the stage your body is going through. In some ways, these stages are similar in both boys and girls. In other ways, they're very different. You should know about both.

© MacDonald Photography/Envision

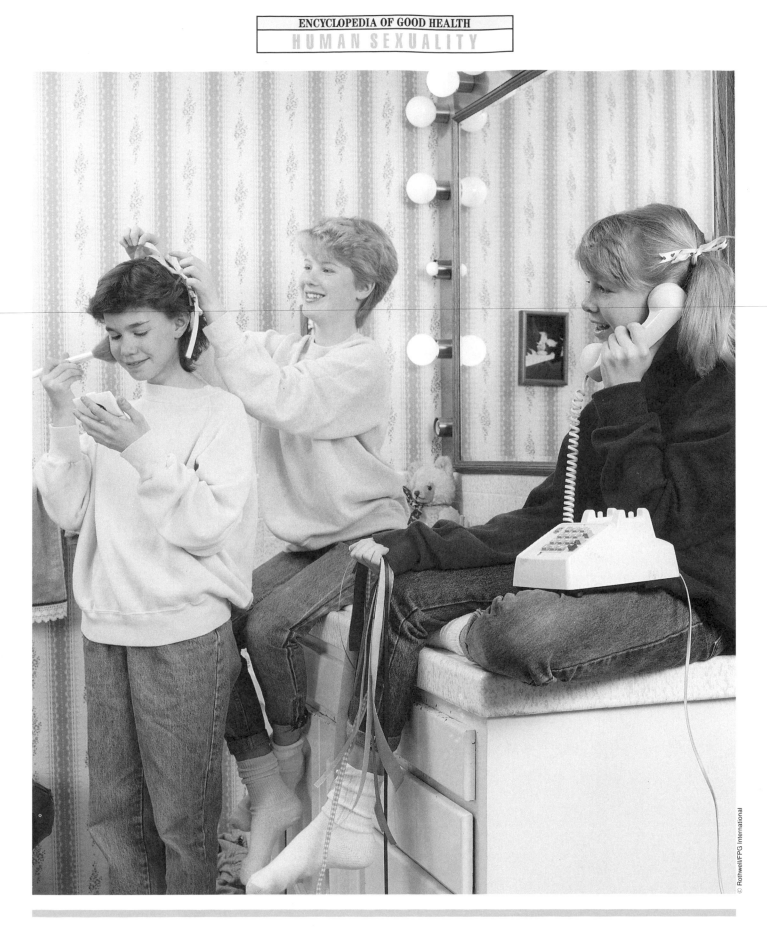

Q. *What are genitals?*

A. Genitals are your reproductive organs—mostly the organs on the outside of the body. Boys and men have a penis and scrotum and girls and women have a vulva, where the vagina and clitoris are located (see page 15).

Separating the Girls from the Boys

You've known for some time that girls and boys have different genitals. Until recently, however, your male and female classmates have been physically similar. In fourth grade, you probably couldn't tell a girl's waistline from a boy's. When you were eight, you and your friends didn't worry about mustaches or menstrual cramps.

Now your friends are changing before your very eyes. The girls seem to develop new curves overnight. The boys aren't short and knobby-kneed anymore; they're taller, and they have hairy legs. As the guys become more muscular and tougher, the girls get rounder and softer.

You can see the physical differences, but you can't see or even feel what is happening to cause them. The process starts in the brain, where the pituitary gland is located. This gland produces several hormones that keep you growing at a slow but steady rate. When you reach a certain age—in girls, it's generally eleven to fourteen, in boys, twelve to fifteen—the pituitary gland increases the production of certain sex hormones. These hormones act as messengers, traveling through the bloodstream to your sex glands.

Girls and boys have different sex glands, or gonads. If you're a girl, you were born with ovaries, located inside your pelvic region. If you're a boy, you've always had testes, or testicles. The testes are located in the scrotum, the pouch of skin hanging below your penis. When those hormones from the pituitary gland reach your gonads, they give them the signal to begin work. What work? The ovaries and testes make their own hormones, which in turn signal all the physical changes that will make you a woman or a man.

Genitals

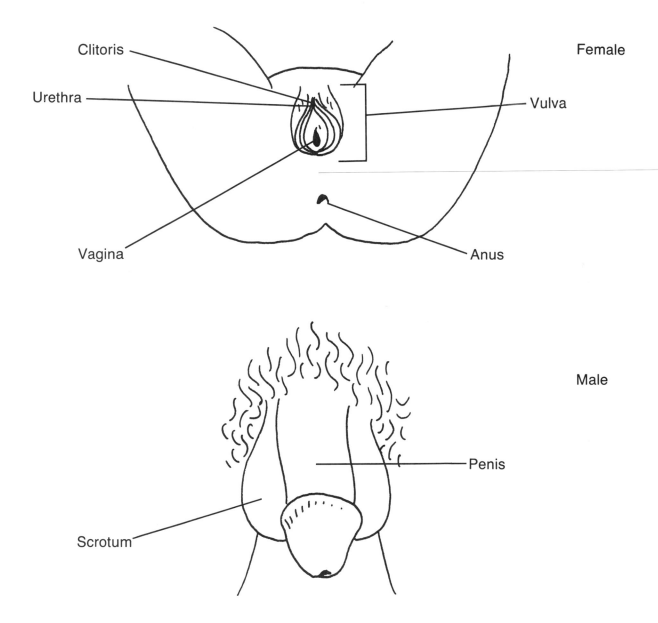

Q. *What are hormones?*

A. Here we refer to hormones simply as body chemicals, but hormones are anything but simple. In fact they're so complex that even scientists don't fully understand hormones.

For your purposes, however, here's what you need to know about hormones: They come from glands in the head, neck, and other parts of the body. There are scores of different hormones in the body, and all of them have a different function. Some control growth and development. Some see that the food you eat is used for energy. Some enable you to produce babies. Still others cause your heart to beat faster and your hands to sweat when you're nervous (see Stress and Mental Health).

The way hormones work together to keep us healthy is amazing. We're quite unaware of them until something goes wrong. And sometimes hormones do cause problems. People who don't grow to normal size (dwarfs), for example, have a shortage of growth hormones. In rare cases forms of physical and mental retardation are caused by insufficient levels of another hormone from the thyroid gland. Hormone activity can also cause more common, day-to-day discomfort. Premenstrual tension, also known as premenstrual syndrome, a problem for some menstruating women, is the result of rising and falling levels of sex hormones (see "A Guide to Menstrual Problems," pages 70–72).

From Girls to Women

Once stimulated by hormones from the pituitary gland, ovaries make their own hormones, one of which is estrogen. When a girl reaches puberty, estrogen triggers physical changes. Different girls reach puberty in different ways, but there is a basic order of stages. Don't worry if your stages aren't exactly as we have them here: This isn't what's *supposed* to happen, it's just a general guide to let you know what to look for.

Stage 1: The most obvious sign that a girl has reached puberty is the development of her breasts. When a girl's breasts first begin to mature, they're no more than bumps beneath the nipples, but they may feel tender because they're developing. Eventually the "bumps" become larger and rounder, and the nipples and areolas get larger (see the Q&A on page 20). While some girls develop full breasts quickly, others' don't mature for a few years.

In our society breasts are considered to be attractive, distinctive body parts. Breasts also play a practical, fundamental role: As mammary glands, they're capable of feeding babies with self-made milk after pregnancy.

Stage 2: Estrogen causes other things to happen, too. At first, straight hair will start to grow around your genitals. Then some time between Stages 2 and 3, it will get coarser and curlier. You may also notice more hair on your legs. All this time your skin gets a little softer, smoother, and oilier. Unfortunately, the increase in oil production promotes pimples (see "Pimple Problems?" pages 18–19).

Stage 3: Many girls experience a growth spurt during puberty. Some girls reach their full height within two years after menarche, the beginning of menstruation (see "The Mechanics of Menstruation," page 22). Other changes: The hips get wider and develop an extra layer of fat to protect pelvic organs. Shoulders get wider, too.

Stage 4: As you can see, most of the changes during puberty are reproductive ones—they ready females for a time when they may decide to have children. A female is never physically capable of having a baby, however, until her menstrual periods begin, usually when she's between the ages of twelve and fourteen or in Stage 3 or 4. However, menarche may occur as early as age eight or as late as sixteen (see "Early Bloomers, Late Starters," page 30). Menarche isn't a sign that puberty is over, but it does indicate that the reproductive organs are mature. Once a girl has her first period, her body will continue to change, but many people consider menarche to be the point at which a girl becomes a woman. (For more on menstruation, see pages 67–77 in Part II.)

Stage 5: Hair appears under the arms and perspiration glands become more active.

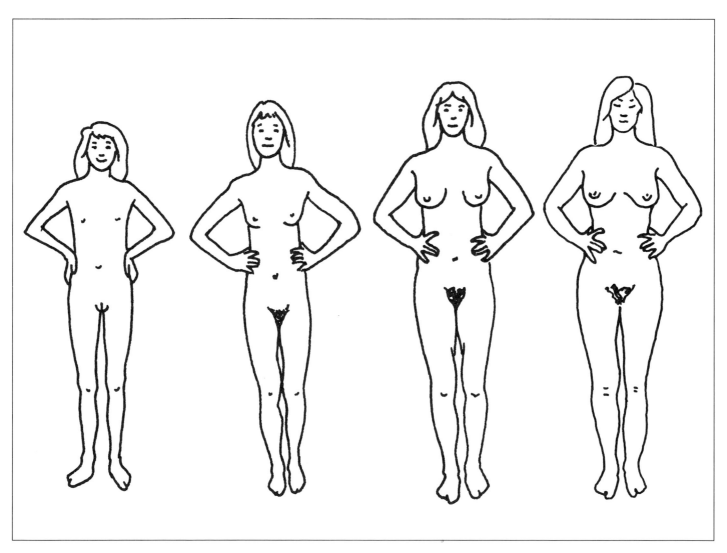

Growing up is a gradual process. At first, you might notice a few hairs near your genitals. Then your breasts will develop a little. Between three and seven years later, you'll have passed through all the first three stages and be a grown woman.

17

Pimple Problems?

You're really looking forward to Friday—the class has been planning a picnic at the lake for months. But on Friday morning, you wake up to find the ugliest pimple you've ever seen on your chin. Why today, you ask your body, when you want to look really good?

In all likelihood hormonal changes have something to do with your pimple. It's called acne: a skin infection caused by oily secretions. Not all teenagers have this problem, but most do notice a difference in their skin during puberty. Some people have serious cases of acne throughout their teen years—even beyond. Others have only mild acne for a year or two, or none at all. It varies from person to person. If you'd like a clue as to how acne may affect you, ask your brothers, sisters, or parents if they were prone to break-outs during puberty. This skin condition tends to be hereditary, so if your mother had only an occasional pimple, you may follow suit.

How do hormones cause acne? They stimulate your oil glands to make excess amounts of a substance called sebum. When this happens, the pores get clogged and a pimple may form on your face, neck, shoulders, upper chest, or back. When the sebum is exposed to air, it turns black and you get a blackhead. If sebum is trapped beneath the skin, you get a white, raised bump, or whitehead. Whiteheads and blackheads can become inflamed and turn red or yellow with pus.

You may not be able to totally cure acne, but you can keep clean and eat well to keep it under control. Here are some easy tips:

○ Avoid wearing make-up (foundation, blusher, powder). Covering up blemishes with make-up only aggravates the condition, but if you like the look of make-up, try some of the medicated cosmetics and flesh-tinted acne creams on the market.

○ Wash your face morning and night. For extra cleanliness, take a bottle of astringent and cotton balls in a little plastic bag to school, or try one of the cleansing products with saturated pads.

○ Wash your hair often—every other day or every day if it's oily. Dirty hair makes for a dirty complexion.

○ Keep your hands away from your face. Just by resting your chin in your hand, you may pass bacteria to your skin. Also, avoid touching your pimples. Not only do you risk infection from dirty hands, you'll also make the pimples look worse. Instead, keep your blemishes clean. If you *have* to "burst" an unsightly pimple that's yellow with pus, wash your hands, wrap your fingertips in a tissue, and use your fingertips (not your fingernails) to gently squeeze, and then wipe the blemish with alcohol.

○ Drink lots of water and eat plenty of fruits and vegetables. What about greasy foods and chocolate? Doctors say chocolate doesn't cause acne, but fatty foods could increase your production of sebum. If any unhealthy foods seem to prompt pimples, avoid them (see Nutrition).

○ Get plenty of sleep and exercise. Try to lower your stress load (see Exercise and Stress and Mental Health).

○ See a dermatologist if your acne is serious.

Almost all male teens have some acne. It is slightly less common in teenaged girls, who tend to develop acne problems only around the time of their menstrual periods.

Q. *What are nipples and areolas?*

A. Nipples are the slightly raised areas on the chest, ranging in color from light pink to brownish black. They're surrounded by a ring of skin, called the areola. During puberty, girls' nipples and areolas swell as the breasts develop. Boys' areolas get larger during puberty, too. Sometimes they even feel a little tender, like girls' do.

The Female Anatomy

Vulva: The entire outer genital area

Vagina: Where menstrual blood passes; this is also where the penis enters during sexual intercourse and where babies pass out of a mother's body

Clitoris: The female sexual organ, located in front of the urethra

Urethra: Where urine passes

Anus: Where solid wastes pass

Uterus: Where menstrual blood comes from and where babies develop

Ovaries: Where human eggs, or ova, are stored

Fallopian Tubes: The path that an egg takes from the ovary to the uterus during the menstrual cycle

Cervix: The passageway between vagina and uterus

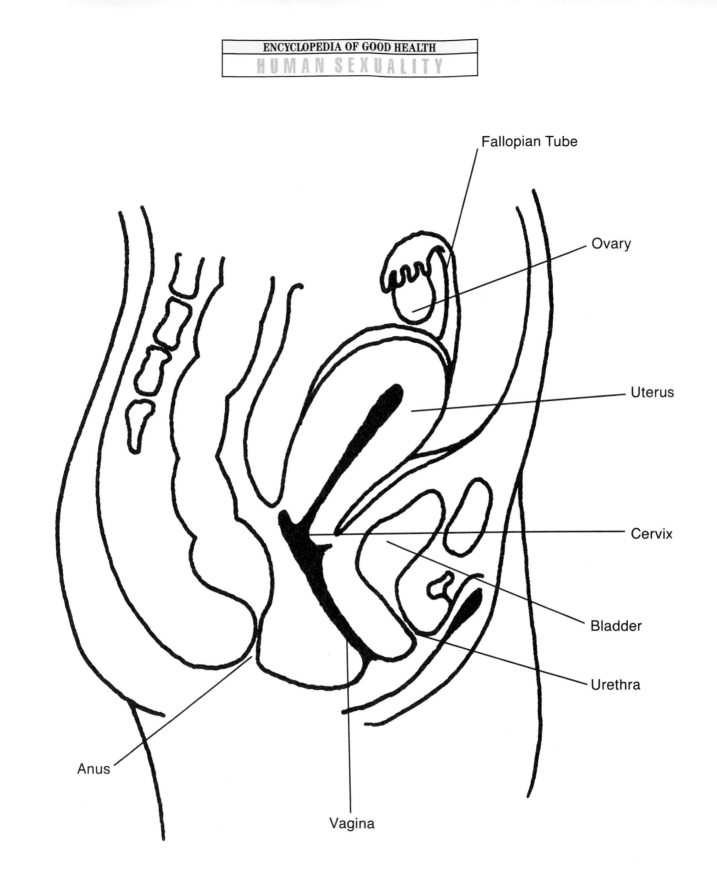

Fallopian Tube

Ovary

Uterus

Cervix

Bladder

Urethra

Anus

Vagina

The Mechanics of Menstruation

If you're a girl and you haven't had your first period yet, don't worry—you soon will. When you do get your period, you'll know because blood will pass out of your vagina. The bleeding will last three to seven days, then stop. About a month from the time you first began to bleed, you'll begin to bleed all over again. This is a cycle you'll follow for many years to come, unless pregnancy, sickness, or other problems interfere (see "A Guide to Menstrual Problems," pages 70–72).

You may be surprised by your first period, but a whole lot happened before you even started to bleed. First of all, you were born with hundreds of thousands of undeveloped ova, or human eggs, inside your body. These eggs are stored in tiny sacs, called follicles, in your ovaries. On page 14 you read that hormones from the pituitary gland stimulate the ovaries during puberty. When that happens the eggs begin to grow and develop. At the same time the ovaries make their own hormones, one of which is estrogen.

As you know, estrogen travels to different body parts, signaling all the physical changes we've discussed: breasts, hair, perspiration glands, etc. These changes evolve gradually, as the pituitary gland continues to send hormones down to the ovaries. Meanwhile, the eggs inside the ovaries keep growing.

Finally, one of the eggs, called an ovum, in one of the ovaries becomes ripe enough and pops out of one of the ovaries (scientists believe the ova-ries take turns producing an ovum each month). This is called ovulation. Does it hurt? Some girls feel a slight twinge or dull ache, but most of us never know this is happening.

As you can see by the illustration, ovaries are located near the fallopian tubes. When the ovum pops out of one of the ovaries, the fringed ends of the tube pull the ovum in. Gradually, the ovum moves down the tube, toward the uterus. Now, while the ovum was getting ready to leave the ovary, hormones were working on the inside of the uterus, making it thick with new blood vessels and spongy tissue. Why? Because for the first of many months to come, your body was readying itself for a baby. The extra blood and tissue is intended to nourish a baby in the uterus.

If sexual intercourse takes place during this time, and a sperm meets up with the ripe egg, the female becomes pregnant. (More on this: page 54.) However, if the egg makes its way through the fallopian tubes without meeting a male sperm to fertilize it, the egg will die after it reaches the uterus. Then, the built-up uterus lining isn't needed anymore. Hormone production drops off and the extra blood and tissue breaks down and falls out of the body, through the vagina. That's what you actually see when you begin to bleed: the lining of the uterus.

At first the blood and tissue come out fast, but after a day or two it slows down. By the time the bleeding stops, the hormones are already working on your next period. About two weeks after the first day you bled, ovulation will occur again.

The Monthly Female Reproductive Cycle

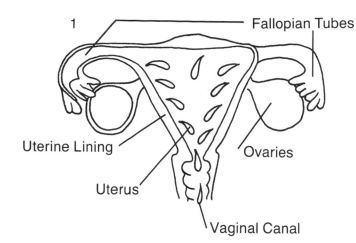

1

Fallopian Tubes

Uterine Lining

Ovaries

Uterus

Vaginal Canal

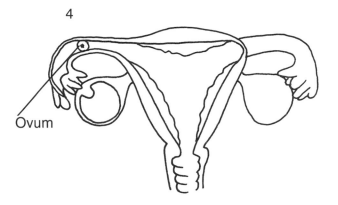

4

Ovum

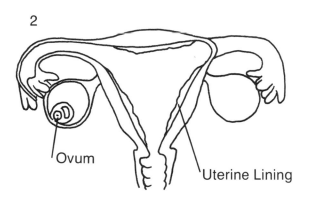

2

Ovum

Uterine Lining

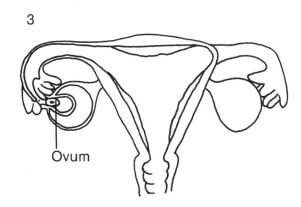

5

Uterine Lining

3

Ovum

(1) On the first day of the cycle, you bleed.

(2) About three to six days after you first bleed, you stop. Meanwhile, the eggs in your ovaries (ova) grow and the uterine lining starts to get thick with blood again.

(3) About fourteen days into your cycle, one of the ovum matures and pops out of the ovary.

(4) The ovum makes its way through the fallopian tube.

(5) If the ovum doesn't meet a male sperm on the way to the uterus, it will die and fall into the uterine lining. By the twenty-eighth day or so, the lining is fully developed and begins to shed. The cycle begins again.

T_F True or False?

Each month the total amount of menstrual blood passed out of the female body amounts to about four to six tablespoons (60–90 ml.).

True. Doesn't sound like enough, does it? The discharge may look like a lot more, but it's less than you think. Of course the amount varies from woman to woman, just as the length of every woman's cycle is different. Most menstruate every twenty-eight days, but it can range from every thirty-one to every twenty-five days.

It's also important to know that when you have your first period, it doesn't "gush out" or catch you totally off guard. Rather, menstrual blood dribbles out. In fact, your first periods will probably be very small. You may not even realize you're menstruating until you go to the bathroom.

Other helpful information: Only half of the menstrual discharge is blood. The rest is excess substances—cells, mucus—from the uterus. The blood stains these substances, which makes them look very red. There's nothing to be alarmed about.

Does menstruation go on for the rest of my life?

A. No. When you get to be about forty-five to fifty-five, your ovaries will stop making some hormones and stop releasing eggs. This change, called menopause, happens gradually. A woman might miss a period or two, then start again for a couple of months. When a woman stops having periods for six months, she can no longer get pregnant.

From Boys to Men

A few years before any signs of puberty appear in boys, hormones from the pituitary gland travel to the testes, located in the scrotum (see illustration). Just as the females' ovaries make their own hormone, estrogen, the testes make their own, testosterone. As you get a little older, hormone production increases. Testosterone signals the different parts of the body to grow and develop.

Like females, males may notice any of the puberty changes first, but often boys your age follow a basic pattern. Don't be alarmed if you veer off the path somewhat and find some of these changes out of order. This is just to give you a general idea of what to expect:

Stage 1: Many boys notice that their penises and scrotums begin to grow. During childhood a boy's scrotum is drawn up close to his body. But when he reaches puberty, the testes inside the scrotum start to hang lower. Then the penis gets longer and wider and the skin around these organs gets darker.

Stage 2: Boys also start to grow pubic hair during the early part of puberty. This comes about similarly in both boys and girls. At first you might notice only a few straight hairs, usually around the base of the penis. As the genitals get larger, darker and curlier hair appears on the scrotum itself, the lower abdomen, thighs, and anus. This usually begins to happen between Stages 3 and 4.

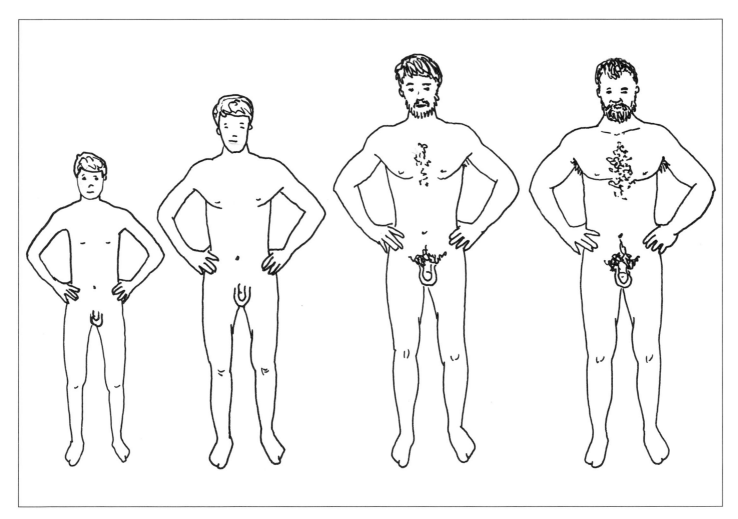

Like females, males pass through various stages on the way to maturity. These changes may begin anywhere between ages ten and fourteen, and end anytime between ages sixteen to twenty.

Stage 3: At this point, ejaculation usually becomes possible. Boys might be surprised to wake up with a thick, white, sticky substance on their bedsheets or shorts. (For more on this, see "Erections and Ejaculation," page 28. Also see "What are semen and sperm?" page 29.)

Stage 4: While girls' bodies become rounder and softer during puberty, boys' get more muscular. Their shoulders get broader, their arms and legs get thicker, and they add inches to their heights. All this time the skin changes: Hormones make the oil glands all over the body work harder. As a result, hair gets dirty quicker, acne may develop on the face, shoulders, chest, or back, and the genitals may feel moist (see "Pimple Problems?" pages 18–19). Hormones also increase perspiration, the origin of new odors coming from the underarms, genitals, and feet.

Stage 5: Hair begins to grow under the armpits. You'll notice that boys' hair on the arms and legs gets darker and thicker, too. Some males get chest and back hair.

Stage 6: Puberty causes the male voice to change. When testosterone reaches the larynx, or voice box, it makes the vocal cords get longer and thicker, changing the tone of the voice. The earliest signs of voice changes actually take place between Stages 2 and 3, but it doesn't happen overnight. At first you may sound a little hoarse, but you'll notice a marked change when you reach the latter stages of puberty.

Stage 7: Finally hair grows on the face, beginning with the corners of the upper lips, gradually spreading across the upper lip, the sides and upper part of the cheek, just below the middle of the lower lip, and finally, on the chin. Remember this varies from person to person. Many men don't develop their full facial hair until ten years or so after they have completed puberty.

© Blumebild/FPG International

The Male Anatomy

Penis: The male sexual organ, and where the urethra is housed

Scrotum: Where the testes are stored

Testes: Where the hormone testosterone and sperm are made

Urethra: Where urine and semen pass

Anus: Where solid waste passes

Bladder: Where urine is collected

Vas Deferens: Tubes that carry sperm from the testes to the penis

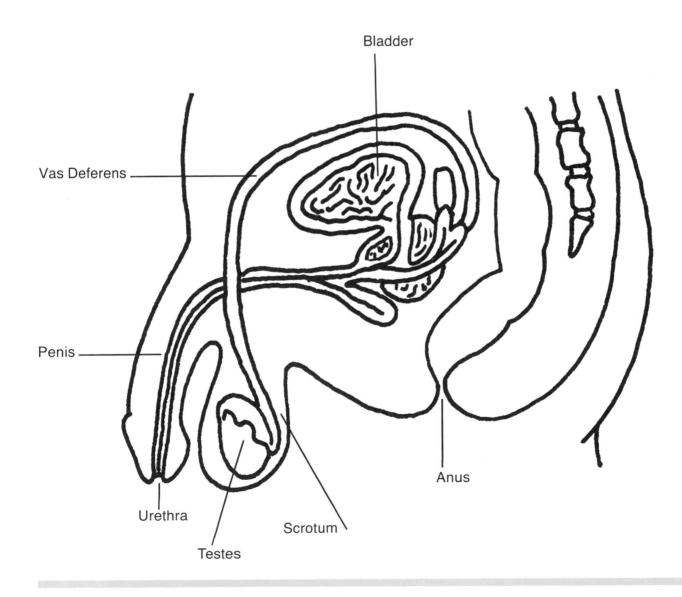

Erections and Ejaculation

For girls, menstruation may be the most significant puberty change. For boys it could be the way their sex organs begin to behave. For example, males of all ages—even babies—can have an erection, but boys going through puberty are likely to have frequent erections. You might be concerned the first few times this occurs, but it's natural and happens to all males. Erections occur when blood rushes to the penis and muscles at the base of the penis tighten. This makes the penis stand erect and get longer and wider. An erection is necessary for sexual intercourse (see page 43) and is usually the result of physical contact.

When boys enter puberty, however, they're sometimes embarrassed to realize their penises become erect without actual contact or even *thoughts* of sex. These are called "spontaneous erections" and are nothing to be ashamed or scared of. All men experience them; erections are a natural part of growing up.

What can you do about a spontaneous erection? If you're in a public place, not much. Some boys cope by getting their thoughts off whatever might have prompted the erection. If you don't touch or rub the penis, the erection will subside.

Sometimes erections lead to ejaculation. When a man ejaculates, the muscles of his penis contract and a white, milky fluid (semen) is pumped out of the testicles and through the urethra in spurts (see illustration and Q&A on page 29). During sexual intercourse, a chain of physical events usually causes a male to ejaculate (more on sexual intercourse, page 43). But when a boy or man brings himself to ejaculation by physical contact, it's called masturbation.

Another occurrence associated with male puberty is "wet dreams." While boys can have erections at any age, an ejaculation isn't possible until puberty, when the testicles begin to make sperm (see the Q&A on page 29). Usually a boy has his first ejaculation around the age of thirteen or fourteen. Masturbation may cause this ejaculation (see page 45) or it may come as a result of a nocturnal emission, also known as a wet dream. What happens: A boy simply ejaculates during his sleep and wakes up to find a little semen on his sheets or in his shorts.

What causes wet dreams? Doctors say it's the body's way of relieving the testicles of built-up sperm.

Q. *What are semen and sperm?*

A. Semen is the thick, creamy, white fluid that passes out of the penis during ejaculation. It amounts to about a teaspoon (5 ml.) and comes out in about three or four spurts.

Every time a male ejaculates, his semen is made up of millions of sperm. Sperm is the father's cell necessary for reproduction. The female's cell is an ovum (see "The Mechanics of Menstruation," page 22 and "How Does a Female Get Pregnant?" page 54). If you could look at a sperm through a microscope, it would resemble a tadpole, with a round head and a long tail. While a female is born with all the ova (eggs) she'll ever have, the male body is constantly making new sperm. The four-to-six week process is a complicated one, beginning in the testicles and moving through several tubes in the genitals until the sperm is ejaculated.

Sperm isn't the only substance that's in semen, however. In fact, only about one-tenth of your semen is sperm. The rest is a fluid made by a gland inside the male body, near the bladder. This fluid helps sweep the sperm through different tubes and out of the urethra during ejaculation.

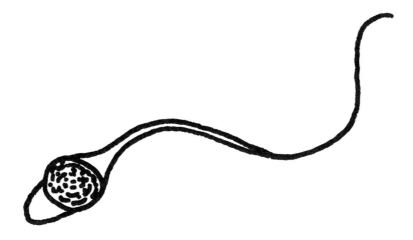

arly Bloomers, Late Starters

Why is it that some girls begin menstruating at age ten, but others don't until they're fifteen or so? The same thing happens among junior-high boys: Some twelve-year-olds worry that all their friends will grow up before they will, while other twelve-year-olds already have deep voices.

Sound familiar? The fact is, it's natural for some people to enter puberty earlier or later than others. Most girls have their first periods between their eleventh and fourteenth birthdays, but some have them when they're eight and some when they're sixteen. Boys tend to begin their puberty changes when they're twelve or thirteen, but some start at ten and others at fourteen.

While the *beginning* of puberty is confusing for people your age, the progress of puberty is also misunderstood. Some people think that a girl or boy who starts puberty early will develop faster than everyone else. But just because a girl begins to develop breasts at age nine is no indication that she'll be a full-grown woman before everyone else is. Early starters may have adult bodies in only two years, or it could take them as long as five years to mature. The same is true for people who are late starters. You may know someone who didn't begin puberty until he was fourteen, but who knows when he'll finish going through all the stages of puberty? Maybe he'll catch up with everyone who started at eleven, or maybe he'll stay two or three years behind.

There's nothing you can do about the uncertainty of puberty, but that doesn't make it easier on people who are going through it. Maybe you're embarrassed to be the first boy in the locker room with pubic hair, or maybe you're humiliated that you're fifteen and you still have the body of a ten-year-old. If so, you're not alone. Ask any adult and he'll tell you stories about his own discomfort during puberty. It's not unusual for you to feel funny about your body, but try not to let it bother you. You'll come along, sooner or later. Part II of this book will help you deal with your insecurities.

One thing you should know: If you're going on seventeen and haven't begun to menstruate yet, or if you're a fifteen-year-old boy and you haven't seen any signs of puberty, it might be wise to check with a doctor. Chances are you're just fine. Still, you'll want to be sure that everything is in proper order. That also goes for early-early starters: If you were already head-long into puberty changes when you were eight or nine, it would be smart to make a doctor's appointment.

T_F True or False?

Your feet bones reach their adult size before you reach your adult height.

True! During puberty the bones in your feet grow faster than your other bones. Because some people your age already have adult-size feet before they're actually adults, they worry that their feet will continue to grow as they continue to grow all over. But don't worry: Your feet will stop getting bigger before you finish getting taller.

T_F True or False?

Girls grow faster than boys.

False. When girls are eleven or twelve, they often find they're taller than boys their age. As you know, boys *and* girls add inches to their height during puberty—as much as four or more inches (10 cm.) in a year, maybe. However, girls tend to begin this growth spurt a couple of years earlier than boys. When boys are thirteen or fourteen, they begin to grow and they continue to grow longer than the girls do. Consequently, boys usually catch up with and get even taller than the girls.

Your Moods, Feelings, and Perspectives Are Changing, Too!

"I don't believe this," Allen's mother said late one Saturday morning. "It's almost noon, and he's still sleeping! Kids are getting lazier every day."

If Allen's mother were to think about it, though, she'd understand why her son seems more tired than usual (even if she wishes he would get up and mow the lawn). At thirteen, Allen is slowly but surely growing up. This means that his hormones are racing around his body, encouraging all the changes that will make him a man. Allen is in a transition phase, so it's no wonder that he needs more sleep. All these bio-chemical processes taking place in his body demand a lot of energy, which also explains why he eats three sandwiches at lunchtime, instead of just one like he used to. After all, food *is* energy, and because these hormonal changes have increased his body's demand for nutrients, Allen should be sure his diet is healthy (see Nutrition).

It's easy to understand how puberty affects young people like you and Allen physically through fatigue and hunger. It's not so easy to understand the emotional changes. While hormones are partially responsible for the ups and downs of adolescence (in a very complex way, hormones can be linked with moods), the main problem is you're in a "limbo land." There's a tug-of-war between childhood and adulthood going on, and you're one of the key players. Read the following stories, and you'll see what we mean.

It's natural for you to sleep more than usual during this time in your life. Your body is working overtime to accommodate the way it is growing.

You want to be independent, but you also need support.

Rosemary is mad because her mother won't let her go to the mall alone. "I'm so tired of you telling me what to do," she fumes. "I am old enough to take care of myself. Why don't you just stay out of my life?"

Rosemary doesn't really mean it, though. Just the other day she had a doctor's appointment. Her mother pulled the car up to the office, stopped, and waited for Rosemary to get out. "I'll be back to pick you up in an hour or so," her mother said. "You're not going with me?" Rosemary's bottom lip trembled. *"Mom, please, you have to go in. Don't leave me here by myself!"*

It's only natural for Rosemary to feel that she's ready to be treated as an adult. After all, her body is growing up. But just when she's called on to perform an "adult" act, like going to the gynecologist for her first pelvic exam, she crumples. You can understand why, can't you? Just because you're developing a mature body doesn't mean you're ready to stride right into the adult world. (By the way, Mom's confused, too. She wants to keep Rosemary close to her, but she knows she also has to let her grow up. Puberty is not easy for parents, either.)

Conflicts with parents are inevitable. You're determined to assert your independence, yet you need your parents' emotional—and financial—support. Young people seem to have the most trouble with parents (and vice versa) between ages thirteen and sixteen.

You have mixed feelings about the way your body is changing.

When Glen first noticed curly pubic hair growing around his penis, he didn't know whether to shout about his good fortune or to hide his early manhood. He was the first boy in his fifth-grade physical education class whose penis began to grow noticeably longer, and the other boys never let him forget it. Now his new black hair would probably call even more attention to him. When the other boys kidded him, were they making fun of him, or were they envious? Instinct tells Glen he should be proud, but he isn't ready to deal with this change—especially since, so far, he's going through it alone.

Shannon has a somewhat similar problem. Although she wasn't among the first in her class to begin menstruating, she was surprised when she went to the restroom at an amusement park and found blood on her underwear. At first, she was excited about telling her mother, but when she got home, she cried. "Why are you upset?" her mother asked. "I thought you were looking forward to this." Shannon didn't know how to answer: Suddenly, she felt depressed that her childhood was gone.

One minute you're up, the next you're down. Changes in your body chemistry as well as the conflicting pressure you get from friends, family, and society affect your mental outlook. It's important to remember that you're not alone in this. Talk to your parents and friends.

What Glen and Shannon are going through is by no means unusual. Who doesn't feel a little pressure at being different from others? You've probably guessed that Glen's friends were actually envious of his changes, but that didn't stop them from teasing him. Now more than ever, he feels vulnerable to what people say about him. He's not sure how he feels about himself, not having adapted to his changes yet, and it's embarrassing to have other people comment.

Shannon really doesn't know how to react, either. Unlike some physical changes, a girl's menstrual period occurs without notice. Who wouldn't have a hard time adjusting to that? Of course, Shannon notices other changes in her body, but menstruation is the final proof that she's growing up. Sure she's happy about it, but many girls also feel a little sad. It's not as if she'll have to behave as an adult today. But menstruation is a big change to get used to.

When Shannon and Glen are twenty-five, they'll still have problems. But they won't be experiencing the rapid physical changes they're dealing with now. People your age have a different kind of stress to cope with compared to someone who's four or someone who's forty. This isn't bad news. It's just good to understand that if you *do* begin to cry or feel "lost" for what seems to be no reason, there's no reason to think you're losing your mind (see Stress and Mental Health).

Don't be surprised if your parents are befuddled by your behavior. Even if they do understand what you're going through (and not all parents do), they don't always know how to help.

Your friends and family are more important to you, but they're also more trouble.

Vince doesn't know when he first realized his mom had a problem with alcohol, but maturity is beginning to weigh heavily on him. He sometimes wishes he could be a little kid again. Then he not only didn't realize what was happening, it wouldn't have worried and hurt him so much. But now he's older and wiser, and it's more difficult to ignore his mother's moods and excuses. Plus, his love for her has changed. When he was younger, she was just Mom and he took her for granted. But as he grows up, his emotions are stronger, more adult. But on top of all this, he's still just a junior-high student, a kid who really doesn't know how to help her.

Kitty is miserable. It's not that Dottie is such a good friend. Everyone knows she says lousy things behind people's backs, then acts real nice when she's with them. What's more, she's loud and conceited. But it doesn't matter—Dottie has very popular friends, and Kitty feels hopelessly left out. Her father told her to invite a girlfriend on a family camping trip, and Kitty knows he expects Sherry, her best friend. But Kitty believes she has no choice. If she invites Dottie, maybe she'll become popular, too.

Are these two totally different stories? Not entirely. The common bond is that both Vince and Kitty are caught up in an emotional tug-of-war. What Vince feels about his Mom is very mature. He may not be totally grown up yet, but he's thinking like an adult. But because he's not an adult yet, he feels quite helpless to deal with the problem. (Unfortunately, most adults have a tough time with this one, too. If you'd like some answers, see Substance Abuse.)

Do you think Kitty's emotions are adult-like? Maybe her reasoning is a little less than mature, but she's acting out of insecurity. Puberty makes many teenagers feel unsure about themselves. It's tough to adjust quickly to all these physical and mental changes, so young people need lots of support. Kitty believes popularity will give her this support, and she feels bad that her picture is not all over the yearbook, like Dottie's.

Maybe Kitty is thinking like a child this time, but that's the whole point of these stories: You don't go from babyhood to adulthood overnight. During puberty, you step gradually into maturity. When you're not a kid but you're not a grown-up either, things get confusing. All of a sudden, your feelings are more complex than they used to be, aren't they?

Parents can be friends, too. Even when you do have differences of opinion, it's to your advantage to try to get along. This relationship will last through your teens, and into the rest of your life.

Members of the opposite sex are of utmost interest to you, but you're "all thumbs" when you're around them.

It's hard to explain what Jay feels for Jessica. When they were in Mrs. Barnes's class, he thought she was silly, like most fourth-grade girls. But somewhere along the way, Jessica got pretty and Jay got interested in girls. He wants to talk to her, to make her interested in him, but this is something new to him. He doesn't know how to get her attention without making a fool of himself.

Speaking of emotions, you may have noticed that yours have changed when it comes to boy-girl relationships. Perhaps you already have a girlfriend or boyfriend and know how confusing it can be. On the one hand, it's exciting to be near someone you like so much. It's not like being with an old friend, which is comfortable and pleasant. Having an interest in a member of the opposite sex demands more of your emotions. It's like riding a roller coaster: You're scared, nervous, jittery, but you think you're having a great time. Romantic feelings for the opposite sex are natural and healthy.

On the other hand, this isn't familiar territory, something you totally understand. Like Jay, you don't quite know how to deal with your new feelings. This is another example of how teenagers span the gap between being too old and not old enough. Not that *adults* are able to handle the opposite sex with total confidence, but at least they've had a little more time to sort things out.

© M. Kozlowski/FPG International

When you're attracted to someone of the opposite sex, you'll probably want to get to know him or her better.

You know it's a serious and complicated thing, but you're so curious about sex!

Who should Gwen believe? Her mom doesn't like for her to ask questions about sex, which makes Gwen feel that it is bad. The kids at school, though, talk about sex all the time. Then in health class, Gwen learns about sexually transmitted diseases and teenage pregnancy, which turns her off to sex. But when she's with her boyfriend, Matt, sex keeps popping into her head. What a mess!

No wonder teenagers are so confused about sex! On the one hand, you're getting all these mixed messages: sex is good; sex is bad; sex is dirty; sex is natural; sex isn't worth the hassle; sex is worth risking everything for.

At the same time, you're confronted with yet another "in-between" crisis. As your body matures, it not only makes you look more and more like an adult, you also feel more like one. You may believe that sex at age fifteen causes too many problems; nevertheless, you can't deny that sex is more interesting to you than it used to be.

No doubt you've figured out that simply looking and feeling like an adult doesn't mean you can or should handle an adult responsibility like sex. Here again, this book will help you understand and deal with sex as it applies to people your age. Once you read the facts, you'll decide that sexual intercourse is for mature adults.

Cultural Sex Roles: What Are They?

Why do girls tend to play with dolls or plastic dishes, while boys seem to favor trucks or baseball bats? Why is it that people make fun of boys for crying and girls are sometimes ridiculed for trying to join the football team?

The answer is cultural sex roles. Boys and girls aren't born with these character traits; they learn them. In fact, studies have shown that when a boy is raised as if he were a girl, he displays the personality features we associate with girls, and vice versa.

Sometimes we are consciously aware of how we learn so-called male or female behavior. For example, a little boy may not think crying is "sissy" until his Dad tells him that "boys don't cry." Or a girl may not realize that sitting with her knees apart is unfeminine until she's told to "act like a lady."

Yet scientists say we also pick up on male and female traits in less obvious ways at a very early age. Parents don't always realize it, but they tend to treat boy babies differently from girl babies. Boy babies may get less cuddling and touching, while girls get more affection. For some reason, our socialization teaches us that males should be rougher and tougher and females should be warm and open. Even something as simple as dressing a little boy in blue and a little girl in pink can affect they way we see the sexes.

Are cultural sex roles good or bad? That's an interesting question. Some people are so used to thinking that girls should act one way and boys should act another that they don't like to see changes made. But who's to say girls shouldn't play sports or boys can't be nurses? Maybe if we didn't teach little boys to avoid crying, they would have an easier time expressing their feelings (see Stress and Mental Health). If more girls grew up with an interest in "boy things," fewer adult women would have to rely on men to help them take care of their cars or manage their money, two things typically considered men's concerns.

Maybe cultural sex roles won't cause much of a stir in your generation. These views change all the time. But the next time you find yourself saying that "girls do it this way," or "boys don't do that," you might find it interesting to ask yourself why you see it that way.

Mini-Quiz

1. On your own paper list ten adjectives describing a baby boy. (Examples: Cuddly. Cute.) Now list ten adjectives describing a baby girl.

Are the words you chose for each baby different? How are they different? Why do you think you chose those adjectives?

2. Picture a secretary. Now picture a doctor. An airplane pilot. A nurse. A flight attendant. A truck driver.

Did you think of a woman when you pictured a secretary, a nurse, and a flight attendant? Did you think of a man when you pictured a doctor, an airplane pilot, and a truck driver? If so, why?

3. List some of the things you admire in someone of the opposite sex. (For example, if you're a boy you might write that you admire girls because they're pretty, smart, and they like to laugh at jokes.) Now list some of the things you admire in yourself and your friends of the same sex. (For example, if you're a girl, you might write that you admire yourself and other girls because you get good grades.)

Compare the qualities you wrote about members of the opposite sex to those belonging to your own. How are they different? Do you tend to admire ''traditional'' qualities, such as aggressiveness for boys and politeness for girls? Or would you say you like the same qualities in both sexes? There are no right or wrong answers to this quiz. The object is to explore your personal notions of sex roles.

Sexual Intercourse Is a Very Complex Subject.

What is sex? The term is broad: It refers to the differences between males and females as well as the study of sexual organs. But on an everyday basis, we use "sex" to name the act of sexual intercourse. Webster's Dictionary defines sexual intercourse as "heterosexual intercourse involving penetration of the vagina by the penis." That's about as simple as an explanation of sex ever gets. You're old enough and wise enough, however, to know that sexual intercourse is far from simple. Before we discuss its importance and the responsibilities it involves, let's describe the facts. What happens during sexual intercourse?

© Michael Keller/FPG International

Sure, you're curious about sex. But sex is more than getting married and having sexual intercourse. When you start to get interested in someone, it's fun to spend time with him/her and find out what you have in common.

Q. *What does heterosexual mean?*

A. Heterosexual refers to a person who chooses to have sexual relationships with members of the opposite sex. The word comes from the Greek root "hetero," meaning "opposite." For example, your dad is heterosexual because he preferred a woman (specifically, your mother) as a mate.

As you probably know, not everyone is heterosexual. A small group of people prefer members of their own sex as sexual companions. This is called homosexuality. "Homo" is the Greek root meaning "same." People who are sexually compatible with either males or females are bisexuals, the root "bi" meaning two (see "Homosexuality," page 61).

Sex, Step by Step

According to two well-known researchers, William Masters and Virginia Johnson, sex is a four-stage process involving the mind and body, muscles and skin, glands and genitals. Different people approach sex in different ways, but nevertheless, say Masters and Johnson, these steps are basically the same for everyone.

Excitement Stage: A number of things can set the Excitement Stage into action—a special perfume, a nice kiss, a happy movie—anything that sparks a romantic response in the mind. Meanwhile, the body prepares itself. In women, the vagina becomes moist and enlarged. In men, blood engorges the penis, causing it to become erect (see "Erections and Ejaculation," page 28). At the same time, the skin flushes, heartbeat and breath quicken, and the eyes open wide.

Plateau Stage: At this point, the changes that occur during the Excitement Stage continue and get stronger. The penis grows larger and more erect and in order to accommodate it during the Orgasmic Stage, the vagina continues to swell inside.

Orgasmic Stage: During this stage, sexual partners usually experience an orgasm. At first, it feels like a kind of warmth spreading all over the body, as one's pulse and breathing continue to quicken. Then muscles in the pelvic region begin to contract. In men, these contractions are usually a little stronger than in women, until, seconds later, he ejaculates and releases semen. Women also experience similar muscle spasms in the vagina and uterus, but they do not ejaculate. These contractions may be very strong or very subtle.

Resolution Stage: The sexual organs, pulse, and breathing all return to normal. How long does it take? Doctors say it's relative to how long the other stages took. That is, if it took about twenty minutes to have sexual intercourse, it will probably take about twenty minutes for the penis to become completely flaccid (limp) and the vagina walls to shrink back to regular size. Of course, sexual intercourse can take more or less time, depending on individual preference.

"Where's the kissing and hugging?" you might ask. What you've just read is a clinical view of how sexual intercourse occurs. There is an emotional progression, too. Not everyone follows the standard, dating-love-marriage-sex pattern, but many people believe it is the smartest way to go. You'll find out why later (see "Why Sex and Responsibility Go Hand-in-Hand," page 57).

© Richard Laird/FPG International

Make no mistake: Kissing is fun and it feels good. But don't be surprised if a long bout of kissing makes you want to go further. Be aware of this, and you'll know when to call it quits.

Did You Know...

That the four stages of sex can take place in most any sexual activity? Heterosexual intercourse, for example, involves a man and a woman. During the Plateau or Orgasmic Stage, the male will insert his penis in the female's vagina. To do this, the man may face and lie on top of the woman, or both partners may face each other and lie on their sides. There are other positions that adults try, too, and sometimes they experience all four stages without penetration.

Masturbation is a sexual act, too. Though it is performed by only one person, male or female, on his or her self, the four-stage physical response is basically the same.

T F True or False?

If you masturbate too much while you're young, it will affect your sex life when you're older.

False. Although people used to think that masturbation caused warts on your nose, pimples, pale skin, wet and clammy hands, blindness, insanity, and a number of other adverse conditions, we now know this isn't true. It's also not true that if you masturbate frequently, you'll like it so much you'll prefer it to other sexual activities. Masturbation is a solo act, while sharing sex with another involves hugging, touching, kissing, and other intimate actions. That makes sex with another person very different from masturbation.

Now, it is true that some religious groups and parents oppose masturbation. Perhaps they believe that it's a selfish, unethical act. But physically masturbation is not harmful to you.

The ABC's of Sex

Having sex with another person takes lots of courage, responsibility, and commitment, which is why many people believe you should reach a certain point in your life before you consider entering a sexual relationship. What point is that? It's not possible to give you that answer here. Our job is to give you the facts and then let you decide. Most people agree that sex is a special form of interaction best practiced with a long-term partner whom you trust. Sex in less-than-ideal situations, however, puts you at risk for an unwanted pregnancy, sexually transmitted diseases, and emotional disappointments.

For these reasons, society has set up an ideal pattern for developing relationships. You might be surprised to learn you've been following this pattern all along.

The Dating Game: When boys and girls are in their teens, they usually begin to pair off and do things in couples. Usually they get together to see a movie, bowl, visit the mall, or go to a dance. In the old days, a boy usually asked a girl to "go out" with him. These days, more and more girls are taking the first step and doing the asking as well. Also popular are group dates in which a bunch of girls and boys get together. In some cases, everybody is matched up with someone else. Other times the pairing is less formal, but there's always the opportunity of getting to know a girl or boy better.

Actually, the whole gist of dating is getting to know someone better. Up until the dating age, children have other children as friends, but puberty puts a whole new light on the opposite sex. Dating isn't reserved for teenagers. People of all ages date until they meet someone special (if at all). It could be that one person will interest you and you won't want to date anyone else. Or you may date a lot of people, each for a short time. The important thing is this: Dating is usually the first step of any romantic relationship.

© WM Moriarty/Envision

It can be distressing to see all your friends dating when you're not. Try to remember that it happens to the best of us—and you don't need a boy/ girlfriend to make you whole. The right opportunity will come along— just be patient.

Problems of Dating

If there's one thing that most people can identify with, it's problems of dating; they're about the same from person to person and generation. The top ten:

1. You think you're old enough to date, but your parents don't.

2. You don't think you're *ready* to date, but your parents do.

3. You would like to date, but no one is interested in you.

4. You can't decide between dating one person steadily, or several at one time.

5. You've been dating someone who likes you a lot, but you don't feel the same way.

6. You've been dating someone you like a lot, but he or she doesn't feel the same way.

7. You feel very nervous during dates.

8. You don't know whether or not to kiss on dates.

9. You want to date someone in particular, but you're afraid to ask him or her.

10. The person you want to date is not available. (You see—you're not alone!)

I've Got a Crush on You!

If you've ever had a "crush" on anyone, you probably know already what it is: an intense interest in someone you find attractive. It's possible to develop a crush at any age, but teenagers seem to have them most often. Everybody has his or her own "crush story" to tell: How about the one where an eighth-grade girl is crazy about the junior-high football coach, so she makes a bookmark out of his newspaper photo and periodically sneaks into his office to squeeze his jacket? (It really happened.) Or the one about the thirteen-year-old boy who is infatuated with a rock video star, so he writes her love letters by the dozens?

Having a crush is a normal part of puberty, and it can be a lot of fun: collecting posters of a movie star, treasuring every word that a special boy says to you, saving the soda can that "she" drank from. At the same time, a crush can get out of hand and cause a lot of pain. It's one thing to fall for the boy next door, who thinks you're pretty special, too. It's another to put all your emotions in an impossible dream: the teacher who is too old and too married or the professional tennis player who is miles—and worlds—away. So go ahead and have your crush, but know where fantasy ends and reality begins.

Falling in Love/Dating Steadily: It may take one date, or it may take a year's worth, but at some point, some couples see each other as more than just casual friends and decide to "go steady" or "go with each other." Perhaps they intend to date steadily until they're old enough and ready to marry. Or maybe they just want to see each other "for now." A lot depends on the individuals and their ages. For example, no matter how strongly you may feel about your girlfriend or boyfriend now, you probably know that she or he may not be your last. After all, you have got a lot of growing up and changing to do before you know exactly what you want out of life. On the other hand, if a twenty-seven-year-old decided to go steady with a woman, he's more likely to "get serious."

If two people really care for each other, they'll have a chance to find out while dating. If they don't, they'll eventually strike out to meet other people. Some adults decide to have sex this early in the relationship. But ideally, they do it with lots of thought and talk first (see "Why Sex and Responsibility Go Hand-in-Hand," page 57).

Q. *How do you know when you're in love?*

A. Love means different things to different people. You probably know people who seem to fall in love every other day. But mature love is not usually something that develops in a week. When you were nine, you might have said that you fell in love with six different people in one year. But when you're fifty, you'll probably realize you've only been in love twice during your lifetime.

That's not to say that you as a junior-high student can't and won't have a real relationship. Most adults will admit that they thought they were deeply in love when they were in junior high. Yet most (or perhaps all) of the love you experience today won't compare to the love you'll feel when you're a little older. Because real love, the kind of love that lasts, means getting to know someone inside and out, caring for that person even though you know he or she isn't perfect, and working through problems with that person when the going gets tough. Love is a tough subject. No one can really tell you whether you're in love or not. Only time will tell if it's true.

K-I-S-S-I-N-G

Why is kissing so much fun? You can credit some of it to learned behavior: You see your parents kiss and you know they enjoy it. You see your older sister and her boyfriend kiss for a half hour or more on the front porch. None of the ninth graders are paying attention to the football game, they're all just trying to find someone to kiss on the bus trip home. Everyone is doing it and liking it, so you want to try it, too.

There's also a physical explanation for the kiss' popularity. Some parts of the body are more easily stimulated than others, and the lips and mouth are especially sensitive. There are scores of nerve endings here that send "pleasure messages" to the brain. This is why some people kiss with their tongues, to stimulate a great number of nerve endings inside the mouth. This is called "French kissing."

Q. What is a ''hickey'' or ''passion mark''?

A. A hickey is a reddish or purplish blotch on the skin, made by a sucking kiss that breaks blood vessels in the skin's surface. The sucking makes blood come up to the top skin layers to create this mark.

Young people sometimes kiss for ''sport.'' People pair off at a party, or couples park at the lake. That kind of kissing is fun, but you've got to be careful not to get carried away. The best kind is between people who know each other well and care about each other.

© Grace Davies/Envision

Engagement and marriage: These steps in the relationship pattern have been established for many generations. In your grandparents' day, couples dated, fell in love, married, then moved in together. Today, people may live together for a few years before they decide to get married, if they choose to marry at all.

Although people have different ideas as to whether it's right or wrong to live together and have sex before marriage, one thing is certain: Sex necessitates some serious decision-making by a couple (such as: What if a pregnancy occurs? What steps will we take to prevent the spreading of sexually transmitted diseases?). In order to deal with these decisions and commitments, most people agree that sexual intercourse shouldn't come before marriage or until a trusting, long-term relationship has been developed.

Did You Know..

That half of all teenage marriages end in divorce within five years? Another 25 percent break up later. Teenagers may decide to marry for many reasons, but the main one is pregnancy. In fact, one out of every six brides (of every age) is pregnant on her wedding day. Another big reason why teens often marry is to escape the rule of strict, over-protective parents.

© Michael Keller/FPG International

Why Sex Is Important

It's true that a decision to share sex with someone requires a lot of thought and smart moves. When the time is right, you'll see that sex is a necessary life function and a fulfilling one. Here's why:

Children: With all the commercial attention given to sex, we sometimes forget its basic purpose: Sexual intercourse between a man and woman can produce a baby. This probably doesn't seem too important to you right now, but it may someday (see "How Does a Female Get Pregnant?" page 54).

Emotional Satisfaction: There is a lot to be said for sharing the tenderness and love that sex is supposed to express. For couples in serious, long-term relationships, sex is a very significant act. It allows both partners to give and receive affection. And it doesn't take a scientist to prove that affection is an important part of life.

Physical Release: Because sex involves the whole body—mind, muscles, and organs—a completed sexual act also provides pure physical pleasure. Do you know how good you feel after a great game of basketball? You get a similar kind of thrill when you share a good sexual experience with someone you love.

Is it okay to go out with just one person? Sure, if you really like him or her. But remember that you've got lots of time to get serious, and it might be fun to get to know different people for now.

ow Does a Female Get Pregnant?

On page 22, you read about a woman's monthly cycle ("The Mechanics of Menstruation"). On pages 28 and 29, you learned about the male's ejaculation and sperm (see "Erections and Ejaculation," and "What are semen and sperm?")Now, let's put them together to explain how pregnancy occurs.

First, we'll retrace ovulation. Remember that every female is born with a certain number of ova (eggs) in her ovaries. When a girl begins to menstruate, one of those eggs matures every month, popping through the ovary wall. The ovum then begins its three-to-four day journey through the fallopian tube to the uterus.

While only 300 to 500 ova will actually leave the female's ovaries during a lifetime, one single male ejaculation may contain as many as 500 million sperm. Furthermore, the male body is constantly making new sperm. Yet very few sperm can have the energy and skill to survive the long journey that's necessary to fertilize an egg.

But if a male sperm goes into or near the vaginal opening just before or after ovulation, fertilization (the meeting of the ovum and sperm) is a definite possibility. When the sperm leave the penis, they're energized by the sugary liquid called semen. Unless they're blocked by some sort of birth control, scores of these microscopic tadpole-like beings race up the vaginal canal, through the cervix, and into the fallopian tubes. On the way, many of the sperm die or get caught in vaginal secretions or wrinkles.

Still, many of the sperm live in the female body for two to five days. If by chance, one of them meets up with a ripe egg in the fallopian tube, it will try to bump its way through the egg's tough wall. If it succeeds, fertilization takes place. The fertilized egg finishes its trip down the fallopian tube, dividing to form a tiny clump of cells. About a week after ovulation, the egg buries itself in the uterine wall to begin a nine-month baby development.

Of course, if sperm isn't successful in fertilizing an egg or if sperm isn't available, the ripe ovum will die within a day or two after ovulation. It will fall into the uterine wall to be shed along with the built-up uterine wall during menstruation.

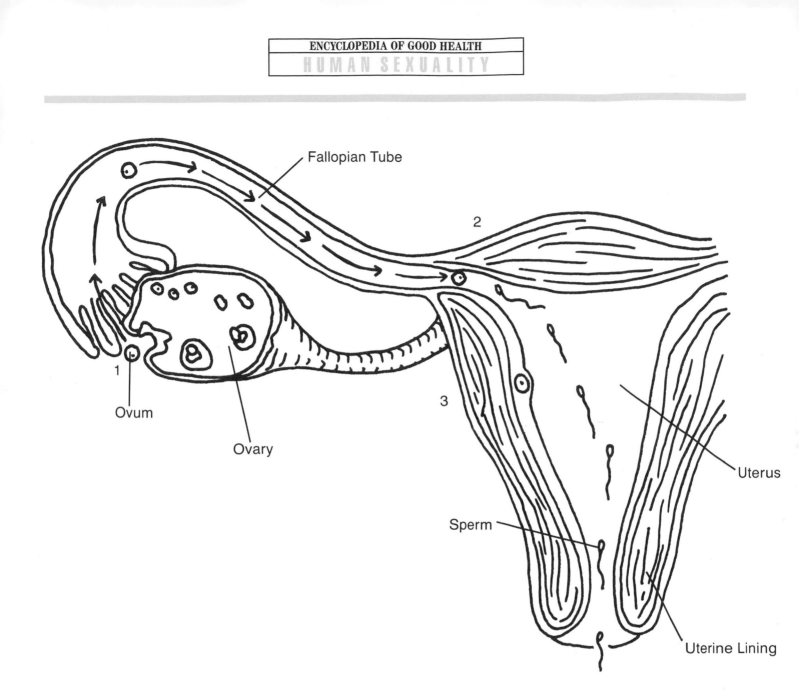

Fallopian Tube

2

1

Ovum

Ovary

3

Uterus

Sperm

Uterine Lining

(1) Once a month, a ripe ovum pops out of the female ovary and travels through the fallopian tube toward the uterus.
(2) After sexual intercourse, sperm swims into the vaginal canal, and—if they can make it there—into the fallopian tubes to meet the ovum.
(3) If the ovum meets up with a sperm, it becomes fertilized and plants itself in the uterine lining. A baby develops from that fertilized cell. If the ovum isn't fertilized, it is sloughed off during a girl's period with the blood of the uterine lining.

Five Myths About Pregnancy

1. *A female can't get pregnant before her first period.*
Ovulation occurs fourteen days before you get your period. So if sperm enters the vagina before a girl begins to menstruate, it is possible for her to become pregnant.

2. *Pregnancy can be prevented if the male pulls his penis out of the vagina before he ejaculates.*
Before the actual ejaculation, some fluid comes out of the penis. That fluid often contains sperm. So even if the male withdraws his penis before ejaculation, it's possible for sperm to enter the vagina. The only sure way to prevent that from happening is to avoid sexual intercourse.

3. *It isn't possible to get pregnant during menstruation.*
Menstrual cycles, especially in a very young woman like you, are unpredictable. One month you may ovulate right on schedule, two weeks after your period began. Then the next month you may ovulate one week or so after your period began. So even if you are bleeding, it's possible that your body is ready for another ovulation. This is why doctors advise against the rhythm or timing method as a birth-control measure. It's difficult to tell when you'll ovulate from month to month so you cannot tell if you are fertile (see page 95).

4. *A female can get pregnant only if she is lying flat on her back during intercourse.*
Not true. As long as sperm enters the vagina, a female has a chance of getting pregnant.

5. *A woman has to have an orgasm to get pregnant.*
It's true that a boy has to have an orgasm to ejaculate, but a girl's orgasm has nothing to do with ovulation or fertilization. Likewise, a male orgasm isn't necessary for fertilization. (Remember Myth number 2.)

Why Sex and Responsibility Go Hand-in-Hand

There once was a father who constantly told his junior-high daughter, "If you take the authority to do something, then you have to take the responsibility for it." What did he mean by that?

Let's say you decide to disobey a rule at school. You should realize that you may get punished or something else disagreeable could happen, and that because you are taking this step on your own, you are taking a risk—a risk you'll have to accept.

Unfortunately, though there are good things about sex, it comes with risks, too. Those risks are complicated for people who are very young and who don't have the stability of a long-term relationship. These risks include:

Unplanned Pregnancies: When pregnancy isn't planned, it can cause problems for most any couple. But pregnancy is probably most unfortunate when the parents are very young and/or not committed to one another. This is why society is so alarmed by the high number of teenage pregnancies and births.

According to Planned Parenthood, these are the most common reasons for unplanned pregnancies: (a) Teenagers either don't know or misunderstand the whys and wherefores of pregnancy and therefore don't use (or misuse) contraceptives. (b) Many teens mistakenly believe that contraceptives are expensive, require a parent's permission, and are difficult to find (see "Where to Get Help," page 111). (c) Unlike adults in long-term relationships, teens tend to have unplanned sex, which means they're not usually prepared with contraceptives. (d) Guilt about having sex or the inability to accept that it "really could happen to me" causes teens to not take the risks seriously (see "Birth Control," page 93).

Sexually Transmitted Diseases: According to Planned Parenthood, teenagers are particularly vulnerable to sexually transmitted diseases (STD's) for these reasons: (a) They don't accept the fact that it *can* happen to them. It's easier to believe, "If I don't think about it, everything will be okay." (b) They're often too embarrassed to buy contraceptives, which can prevent or lower the risk of contracting a sexually transmitted disease. (c) They are usually not comfortable enough with their partners to discuss STD's, which could prevent their spread. (d) There are so many hormonal changes occurring in their bodies that they don't recognize an STD warning sign and don't have the disease treated if it can be. (For more, see "An STD Glossary," pages 88–89.)

Emotional Trials: The question of sex can be an emotional hardship on teenagers. Although their bodies may be ready for sexual intercourse or other sex acts, a young person may not feel mentally equipped to deal with this super-sensitive issue. (Adults don't always know how to handle sex, either.) It doesn't help that teenagers often feel that they don't have anyone to talk to about it. They can't always talk to their parents, who may disapprove. What's more, teens don't usually have the support of their partners. Even if they do, it's likely that the boyfriend or girlfriend is just as inexperienced and unsure.

Because teenage sex is usually a taboo subject (meaning we're not encouraged to talk about it much), young people sometimes feel very guilty when they think about it. Perhaps they feel bad because they know their parents would be upset. Or maybe they personally believe that sex before marriage is wrong. Fear of pregnancy or sexually transmitted diseases could also spur a case of the guilts. Whatever the cause, guilt can weigh heavily on anyone, especially a young person.

Partner Commitment: Having sex with someone doesn't always result in a long-term relationship. Yet, sex can tie two people together for life in several ways. If a disease is passed on through sex, a person will remember the partner who gave it to him or her for a while, if not for medical reasons (the doctor may need to ask him or her some questions), then at least in mind and body. Every time a person has sex with another person, a personal, private, vulnerable part of one's self is shared. A few people are able to have sex without thinking about it too much, but not many. It may be a one-night stand and the partners never see each other again—but memories of the incident will linger. Sometimes those memories aren't so good. And sometimes they come back to haunt the participants. For example, a boy goes too far with a girl in his class. Later, he finds out she's a friend of his girlfriend's. What are the chances that the girlfriend won't hear about it?

Of course, there's always the chance of an accidental pregnancy. Even if the participants don't get married or have the baby together, there will probably still be an emotional impact.

It's no wonder that many people realize how important and demanding sex is. That's why they choose to wait to have sex—instead of sharing it with just anyone.

Did You Know...

That fewer pregnant teenagers marry their babies' fathers than twenty years ago? But long-term studies of the education and earnings of young mothers (married or not) show they are less likely to go on with their education. And while they're more likely to work, these teenagers are less likely to have high earnings. Of course there are exceptions to every rule, but social organizations generally agree that teenage pregnancies and marriages have the odds against them.

© MacDonald Photography/Envision

omosexuality

Most people are heterosexual; they desire persons of the opposite sex for romantic love and sexual relationships.

Thirteen percent of all men and 5 percent of all women in the United States are homosexuals, which means they prefer partners of the same sex. Homosexuals are nothing new in history or culture. They were written about in the Bible and are found in almost every group of people across the world.

Why are some people "gay" or lesbian (a female homosexual) and others are not? That's a good question. At one time, people believed that homosexual behavior stemmed from the way parents treated their children. Others have traced homosexuality's roots to broken homes, a failure at dating the opposite sex, or homosexual friends.

These days, researchers believe that none of these is the true cause. If there is a cause at all, it is a very complicated one. Currently, the leading theory is that homosexuality has something to do with hormone levels during the mother's pregnancy. However, the issue continues to be controversial among doctors, researchers, and everyone else.

What is certain is that homosexuality is one of today's most controversial and misunderstood issues. Some people believe that homosexuals are mentally ill and should not be allowed to live and work in our society. Others believe that homosexuals are just like heterosexuals, except for their sexual preferences. You'll have to decide for yourself how you feel. In any case, you will probably have to think about this issue many times in the future. Even though some people continue to discriminate against homosexuals, they are becoming more and more accepted by society.

Note: There is a difference between being a homosexual and being curious about or attracted to members of the same sex. It is common for children or teenagers to be attracted to members of their own sex, but in most cases these feelings are eventually replaced by heterosexual attractions.

Music videos and news stories often glamorize teenage motherhood. In real life, motherhood is hard work and a lot of responsibility—the baby doesn't go away on Friday night just because there's a party.

What Can I Do To Improve My Understanding of Sexuality?

D oes this seem like a peculiar question? It's not when you consider how trying your teenage years can be. There is plenty you can do to help make this time when you are changing so much a positive experience. One way is to chart your puberty changes so you'll know more about what to expect. You can also bone up on your healthy habits, because feeling good can make all the difference in how hormonal changes affect you.

When it comes to sex, you have to do more than decide to avoid it. In this section, you'll get specific guidelines on *how* to say "no," as well as what to do if you're in trouble. So don't just sit around and let nature take its course. Get interested in how your body is changing, then take charge.

Keep Track of Your Progress

Are you interested in how your body is changing? Why not keep a record? This way you'll feel like you understand what's happening to you. Plus you'll be able to predict what your next changes might be.

Refer back to "From Girls to Women," page 17, "From Boys to Men," page 25. Read through the various stages from puberty and determine about where you stand now. Take a sheet of paper or, better yet, open a notepad or composition book, and begin your journal. Set up a chart like the one below.

BOYS

DATE: _____

HEIGHT: _____

WEIGHT: _____

STAGE: _____

PUBIC HAIR: _____
_____

FACIAL HAIR: _____
_____

OTHER CHANGES: _____
_____
_____
_____

GIRLS

DATE: _____

HEIGHT: _____

WEIGHT: _____

STAGE: _____

PUBIC HAIR: _____
_____

BREASTS: _____
_____

OTHER CHANGES: _____
_____
_____
_____

How to fill in your chart:

1. Write in the date, your height, and weight.

2. Next to "Stage," put an estimate of the stage you think you're in. For example, if your penis is just now beginning to grow longer, you're probably in Stage 1.

3. Next to "Pubic Hair," "Facial Hair," and/or "Breasts," briefly describe your progress. For example, if you have no pubic hair yet, write "none." Next to "Breasts," you might write, "Tender and slightly larger."

4. Next to "Other Changes," write about what-

ever has happened recently: menstruation, ejaculation, pimples, voice changes, body odor, rounder hips, hairier arms and legs, oilier hair and skin, and so.

Every two months or so, fill out a new chart and enter in any new information. By referring back to pages 17 and 25, you can guess what your next changes might be.

You'll enjoy your journal for a few more years, but once finished, why not save it? Because parents and children are often similar in the way they go through puberty, your own kids might appreciate having your progress chart to follow.

NOVEMBER

SUN.	MON.	TUES.	WED.	THURS.	FRI.	SAT.
	1	2	3	☒ 4	☒ 5	☒ 6
☒ 7	☒ 8	9	10	11	12	13
14	15	16	17	18	19	20
21	22	23	24	25	26	27
28	29	30				

For Females: When You Begin to Menstruate

It's also a good idea to keep a record of your menstrual cycles. This way you'll know about when to expect your next period, plus you'll learn about your personal pattern.

Get a calendar specifically for this purpose. On the first day of your bleeding, mark an "X" on your calendar. For every day you continue to bleed, put an "X" on that date. A month or so later, when your period starts again, do the same. Your calendar will look something like the one above.

After you've recorded your period for two months or more, count the number of days that come between the first day of bleeding for each month. For example, if you started on January 1, and again on February 1, then you probably can expect your period to start again thirty days after February 1. The number won't be exactly the same from month to month. In fact, during the first few months your cycle will probably be very irregular. Even so, this system will help you estimate the time of your next period. For example, if you usually begin your period around the fifteenth, then you'll know to put tampons or pads in your pocketbook around the tenth, just in case.

A calendar like this will also enable you to estimate when you ovulate and when to expect premenstrual symptoms, if any. Remember: Ovulation usually occurs about fourteen days after you first begin to bleed. Premenstrual problems—fluid retention, tension, cravings—occur ten days or so before your period.

Develop Good Health and Hygiene Habits

Let's start with the basics. Cleanliness is always important, especially during puberty. Remember that hormonal changes can step up the production of oil in your skin, hair, and genitals. What's more, you perspire more than you did when you were six years old, and that perspiration is taking on a stronger, adult odor. Add these changes to menstruation, ejaculation, and other secretions, and you can see why cleanliness is a must.

Bathe or shower daily, shampoo your hair at least two or three times a week, wash your face morning and night, brush and floss teeth after every meal, and wear an anti-perspirant/deodorant. Change clothes every day—especially your underwear. When you're washing, pay special attention to your genitals and underarms.

Nutrition is another healthy essential. As your body grows and develops, it requires higher levels of nutrients. Neglect these nutrients and you may feel tired, skin may be more prone to break-outs, and in some cases, puberty changes may be delayed. Watch your fat and sugar intake, but load up on fruits, vegetables, lean meats, seafood, poultry, and water (See Nutrition).

Don't forget exercise, either. It not only helps your body do its work more efficiently, it also makes you feel more energetic, helps you look better—both body-wise and complexion-wise—and generally improves your attitude. Girls who menstruate find that exercise helps relieve cramps and discomfort, too (see Exercise).

Because there are so many changes in your life these days, stress management skills are nice to know. Learn to relax and avoid excessive worry whenever possible. Seek the support of family and friends. Exercise helps diffuse stress, too (see Stress and Mental Health).

You're not a baby anymore, and eventually you'll have to depend on yourself to see that you're well cared for. So make these and other common-sense habits a regular part of your life. Now, here are more specific health pointers.

For Females: Menstrual Protection

Have you ever wondered what women did long ago to catch their menstrual flow? They used everything from grass to soft cloths to sponges. But these days, you have all kinds of feminine hygiene products to choose from. The options:

Pads or Napkins: These products are made from layers of soft cotton, which absorb your menstrual blood as it flows out of your body. The very thick pads are for heavy periods, particularly on the first days of your cycle. The thin pads are recommended for light days at the end of your cycle, or even between periods, to catch the cervix's normal secretions.

Today, most pads have adhesive strips, designed to stick to and fit snugly in your under-pants. But some people still prefer older varieties, which are either safety-pinned to your underpants or held in place by a thin elastic belt around the waist.

No matter how heavy or light your flow is, sanitary napkins or pads should be changed at least every three or four hours. This way you'll feel cleaner and fresher, and you won't have to worry about odor. Menstrual blood doesn't smell bad, but once it comes in contact with air it may.

Used pads should be folded, wrapped in toilet tissue, and placed in a wastebasket. Don't flush them in the toilet, as they may clog plumbing. Keep spare pads *clean*. If you carry them in your pocketbook, put them in a little pouch or even wrap them in foil, if you have to. Your vagina is very sensitive, so cleanliness is essential.

Tampons: Napkins and pads catch menstrual blood outside the body, but tampons absorb from inside the vaginal canal. Made from absorbent cotton, tampons have a string attached to the end and are inserted in a few different ways: (1) through a two-piece cardboard or plastic tube that "injects" the tampon; (2) with a stick that guides the tampon in place; (3) or with the finger. Once in the vaginal walls, the tampon expands to absorb blood coming through the cervix. The tampon is removed by pulling the string, which is left dangling outside the vagina.

All tampon manufacturers include a set of instructions for inserting and removing the tampon, but if you have questions, the box "Questions and Answers About Tampons" should help.

Like napkins, tampons come in various sizes. The junior or regular size is recommended for girls your age, but you may graduate to a larger size when your flow is particularly heavy. Tampons should also be changed every three to four hours. Because you can't feel a tampon like you can napkins, tampons can be easy to forget, but by all means, don't leave one in for too long. Not only will a forgotten tampon smell, it can also cause health problems (see "Toxic Shock Syndrome," page 70). When you remove a tampon, wrap it up in tissue and place it in a wastebasket.

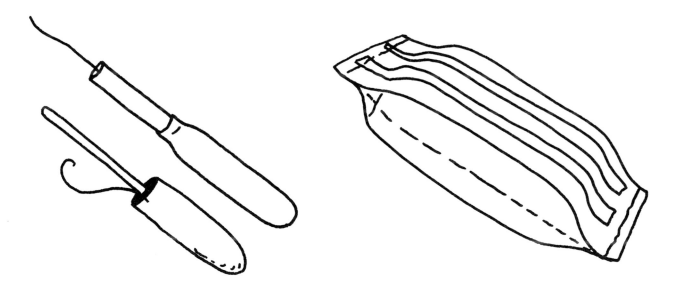

Top left: A tampon, the kind that is inserted via a plastic or paper tube. Bottom left: A tampon inserted with a stick. Right: A feminine napkin.

Q. Questions and Answers about Tampons

Q. Can a tampon get lost inside of me?

A. No. The tampon goes through the vaginal opening and into the vagina, but it stays there. It can't get into the uterus. The opening from the uterus to the vagina, the cervix, is too small for the tampon to pass through.

Q. What do I do if the tampon string gets pushed into my vagina?

A. Just reach your finger up inside and pull the string or tampon out. If that is difficult, squat as if you were urinating. This pushes the tampon lower in the vagina.

Q. Will inserting a tampon cause me to lose my virginity?

A. A virgin is a girl who's never had sexual intercourse, so technically, inserting a tampon will not affect your virginity. However, a tampon may stretch or tear your hymen, the thin skin just inside the opening of the vagina. No cause for concern; although at one time people thought virginity was determined by whether or not the hymen was broken, this isn't the case. In fact, the hymen may be stretched or torn in a number of different ways: by doing an acrobatic split, riding horseback, even falling off a bike.

However, whenever your hymen is stretched or torn, it may bleed a little. But unless it bleeds a lot or hurts, there is no reason to see a doctor.

Q. What if I can't insert the tampon?

A. There are several things you can do. First, try to relax! If you tense up, the vaginal muscles may contract and make inserting the tampon difficult. Try lubricating the tampon with petroleum jelly, but don't use creams or lotions, since they can irritate the vagina.

If that fails, then wear a napkin or pad for a few months and try gently stretching your opening with a finger a few times a week. Eventually, you should be able to get the tampon in.

Toxic Shock Syndrome

If you do use tampons, there is a disease you should know about. It's called toxic shock syndrome (TSS), and it's caused by bacteria in the vagina. Although TSS is very rare—about one in 25,000 women may come down with it during menstruation—the Centers for Disease Control report that two-thirds of the cases involve fifteen to twenty-five-year-olds. Doctors think young women may be particularly vulnerable because they haven't built up an immunity to TSS bacteria, like older women have.

How do you prevent TSS? Be sure to change your tampons regularly, and avoid the super-absorbent tampons whenever possible, since these seem to increase the risk. Doctors also recommend that you cut back on use of tampons by wearing a pad at night.

Symptoms usually start with a sudden high fever, vomiting, diarrhea, and perhaps a sunburn-like rash. What should you do if you notice these symptoms? Remove the tampon immediately and get to a doctor.

A Guide to Menstrual Problems

Cramps: If you are having cramps, welcome to womanhood. Unfortunately, having menstrual periods means that some women—especially young women—have menstrual cramps. Sometimes sharp and severe, other times mild and achy, cramps may occur before or during your period, if at all. The doctors' word for this condition is dysmenorrhea.

Doctors have different theories about what causes menstrual cramps. One of the most popular explanations points to prostaglandins, hormones that help the uterus contract. Women who have problems with cramps have been shown to have more prostaglandins in their bodies than women who don't.

For some reason, young women like you are more likely to have cramps, but the good news is they usually get better with age. In the meantime, follow these tips:

○ Exercise! It helps ease menstrual flow, relieve congestion and constipation, and rid the body of excess water (see Exercise).

○ Massage your lower abdomen, or place a heating pad or hot-water bottle there. This may break up the congestion of blood in the pelvic area, which may also contribute to cramps.
○ Try an over-the-counter pain reliever, such as aspirin or an aspirin-like medicine.
○ If all else fails, see a doctor. The cramps may be a sign of underlying problems, or she may prescribe a stronger medication.

Bloating is caused by fluid retention. The mechanics are that estrogen, an important hormone in the menstrual cycle, interferes with your body's ability to flush out excess water by urination. When this water stays in the body, you feel bloated. It's a minor problem, but if you find it bothersome, try this:

○ Drink lots of water. (It makes your system work harder to get rid of it.)
○ Stay away from salty foods. Sodium also keeps water in the body (see Nutrition).
○ See a doctor if the problem is extreme.

© Sandy Roessler/FPG International

Studies suggest that women who exercise have fewer problems with menstrual discomfort. That doesn't mean you should go jogging whenever you get cramps (although it might help). However, exercising on a regular basis—three to five times a week— will have a positive effect.

Irregular Bleeding: If you "spot" between periods, or if your period comes at different intervals (three weeks apart, then five, and so on), it's probably nothing to worry about. Because your body is just now adapting to womanhood, it may be a few years before you have regular periods. Emotions, poor eating habits, and overwork can affect your period. Between-period bleeding usually happens at ovulation.

However, if you miss a period for a few months, or bleed between your periods, you should see a doctor. Something could be amiss.

Amenorrhea is the abnormal absence of menstruation. There are various reasons why this condition occurs. If you do not eat properly, it may be due to a lack of nutrients. Girls and women who exercise strenuously or who are very thin may stop menstruating, since females have to have a certain level of fat in order to function normally. Amenorrhea may also be the result of glandular problems, ovarian cysts, or other disorders (see Nutrition and Exercise).

Don't be too concerned if you miss one period. Again, this is a common occurrence for girls your age. However, if you have had sexual intercourse and miss your period, or if you miss two periods or more for unexplained reasons, see a doctor.

PMT stands for premenstrual tension. This condition is currently the subject of much debate. Doctors aren't totally sure what causes it. The general belief is that hormonal imbalances during the seven to ten days before menstruation prompt the following symptoms: tension, mood swings, bloating, headaches, and food cravings, among other things.

PMT causes major problems for some women; others have only periodic symptoms. The good news: Women your age usually don't have PMT symptoms. But if you think you do, check with a doctor.

Constipation and diarrhea are often problems before or during menstruation. Hormones probably cause these digestive disturbances, too. Offset constipation by eating high-fiber foods (broccoli, apples, whole grains) and drinking lots of water. Diarrhea will probably subside with rest and time. Drink juice and other fluids to get important nutrients back into your system. Watch out for spicy and other irritating foods and you may be able to prevent this problem. As always, if either of these disorders is serious or recurring, see a doctor (see Nutrition).

Heavy Bleeding: Some months your period may be heavier than others. This is normal for women of all ages. However, if you're soaking through a pad or tampon every hour for a whole day, or if your period goes for five days with no sign of slowing down, it's a good idea to see a doctor.

Facing page
Girls who over-exercise can have problems with missed periods. That's because estrogen—one of the reproductive hormones—is stored in body fat. If your body fat level is too low, it can affect your estrogen production and subsequent menstruation cycle.

T_F True or False?

During menstruation, girls should avoid bathing and exercising.

False. In fact, you are apt to perspire more heavily while you're menstruating, so a daily bath or shower is important. Contrary to some old wives' tales, strenuous exercise won't increase or extend your period, either. Exercise may relieve cramps.

Don't be Afraid of the Pelvic Exam!

Once you begin to menstruate, you'll need to think about having a gynecological exam. A gynecologist is a doctor who treats problems unique to women. For the rest of your life, you'll make yearly appointments with a gynecologist to be sure your system is functioning properly.

Women—especially women your age—usually experience anxiety or fear at gynecological exams. It's understandable to be shy about personal problems with a doctor. But once you realize that a gynecologist is very interested in helping you, sees hundreds of women in a year, and understands your problems and embarrassment, a pelvic exam won't seem bad at all. When it's all over, you'll be glad that you take such good care of your health.

Basically, here's what happens during the exam:

1. The doctor or nurse will talk to you about your periods. At this time, you'll tell her any problems or questions you might have.

2. After you undress, you'll cover yourself with a paper sheet and sit on the examining table.

3. The doctor may chat with you a few moments, then ask you to lie on the table.

4. The doctor will examine your breasts.

5. Next, the doctor will ask you to put the heels of your feet in some special stirrups at the end of the table. This may feel a little strange at first, but it will help the doctor see your genitals better. You'll then "scoot" your bottom down to the end of the table.

6. Very quickly, the doctor will examine your genitals with a finger before inserting a speculum. This is a metal or plastic tool that holds open your vaginal walls. It won't hurt, but you will be able to feel it. Remember to stay relaxed, and this examination will be even easier.

7. While the speculum is inserted, the doctor will give you a Pap test. By gently scraping your vaginal area, the doctor will be able to check you for cancer. (The scrape or swab won't hurt, either.) The doctor won't test for cancer right away. He'll just put your Pap smear away for later examination by special researchers. You'll be contacted only if the vaginal sample is abnormal.

8. A few other minor procedures, such as an anal finger probe, may be performed, but this is the basic exam. Then you'll get dressed and leave.

It's good to talk to your doctor about your examination. If it helps, write down the questions you have ahead of time. Then you won't forget.

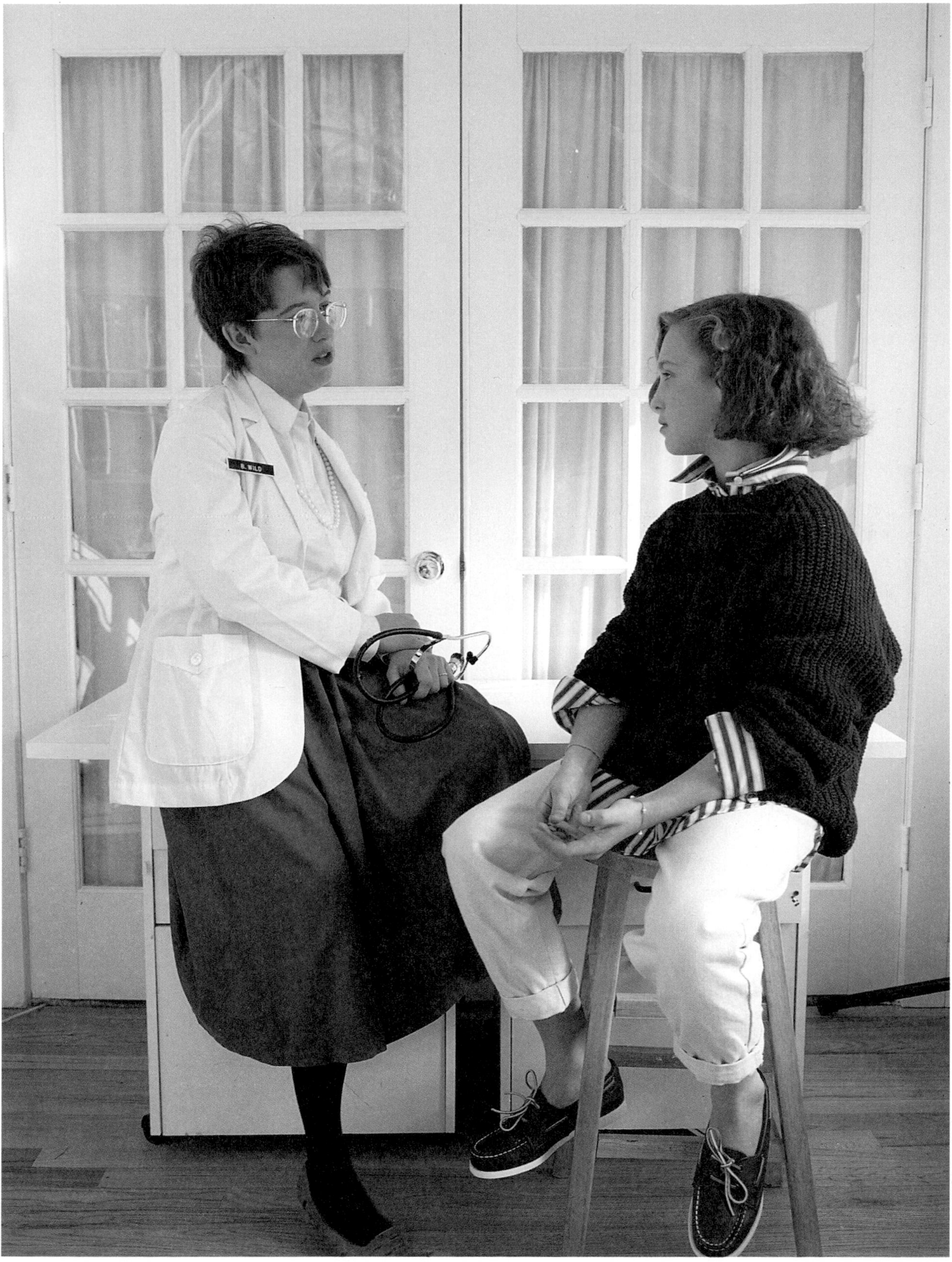

© M. Nelson/FPG International

Breast Cancer and the Self-Exam

Of every eleven newborn girls, one is destined to get breast cancer. Thanks to new ways to find and treat this cancer, though, 50 to 60 percent of these women are saved. Doctors say we can increase that percentage dramatically by taking note of the risk factors and performing breast self-examination.

It's true that older women are more likely to have breast cancer, but you're smart to practice good health habits now. If breast cancer is in your family history; if you began menstruating at an early age; if you have children after the age of 30; and if you eat a high-fat, high-cholesterol diet, you are more likely to have breast cancer someday. In any case, doctors say all women should perform the self-examination after every menstrual period:

1. Do this exam on a regular basis, at least once a month. When you shower is a convenient time to do it.

2. Squeeze each nipple gently and look for discharge.

3. Keeping your fingers flat and together, move around the breasts in a circular motion, checking for lumps, hard knots, or thickenings.

4. Stand in front of a mirror. Put your hands on your hips, tense your muscles, and look at both breasts.

5. Raise your arms above your head and check for dimpling or changes in shape.

6. Lie on your back. Place a pillow under your right shoulder and your right hand behind the head. Moving in a circular motion, feel your right breast gently. Begin on the outside part of the breast until the circle is finished. Then move one inch (2.5 cm.) toward your nipple and in another circle. Continue until your breast has been completely covered. Repeat on your left breast.

If you discover anything extremely unusual, show your mother or doctor.

Here's what to be on the lookout for:

○ Lump(s), especially if painless and only in one breast;
○ Discharge from the nipple, especially if it's bloody and only from one breast;
○ Skin changes such as flaking, crusting, or sores around the nipples.

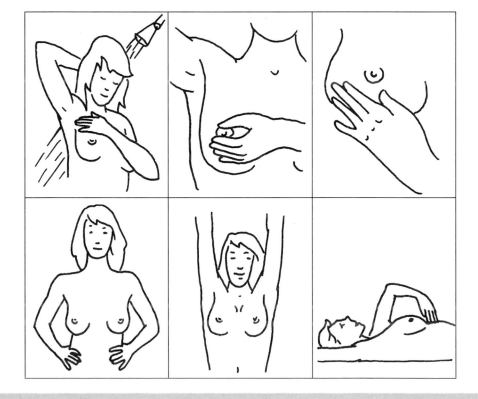

Q. *What do I do if I begin to menstruate at school?*

A. You could begin to menstruate anywhere, anytime, and because you spend a considerable amount of time at school, it could very well happen there. When you get to be about eleven or so, it might be smart to carry a pad in your pocketbook for such an emergency. Blood will not come "gushing out." In fact, your first menstrual period will probably be very light. Still, when you first notice blood in your underpants, you'll want to protect your clothes from further bleeding. If you don't have a pad with you, perhaps your school has a napkin machine or a friend is carrying one in her pocketbook. Or you can always see the school nurse. She'll be sure to have products like this on hand.

If all else fails, tell your teacher that you're ill and ask to go home. He or she probably won't ask any questions.

Vaginal Secretions

Some discharge from the vagina is normal. Like the skin on the outside of your body, the skin on the inside of the vagina constantly sheds dead cells. During puberty, the vaginal walls shed cells even faster, and the vagina makes some fluid to wash them away. A year or two before menarche (your first menstruation) you can expect a clear, white, watery substance from your vagina that leaves a yellowish stain on your underpants. However, some discharges may be caused by various disorders. You should see a doctor when you notice any of the following:

○ A discharge with an unusual or foul-smelling odor may signal a vaginal infection (trichomoniasis and other forms of vaginitis).

○ A discharge with an unusual color—anything too different from the clear, white, or gray discharge you're supposed to have. Abnormal secretions may look thick and curdy (candida vaginitis, commonly known as a yeast infection) or gray-green and runny (trichomoniasis).

○ A discharge unusual in consistency or amount—anything that exceeds what you're used to.

○ Vaginal itching, burning, or swelling could be the clue to pelvic inflammatory disease, vaginitis, urinary tract infection, even a sexually transmitted disease.

For definitions of these various disorders, see the glossary in the back of the book.

For Males: Sexual Health for Men

Throughout life, your sexual organs will go through very gradual changes. Here's what you should know about a few problems:

Urinary Tract Infections can develop in men of all ages. The most common symptoms are pain or burning during urination, a need to urinate frequently, and blood in the urine. You can treat this problem at home by drinking lots of water (several gallons in the first 24 hours) to wash bacteria from the body and fruit juices for the acid and nutrients. If this is a frequent problem for you or if the symptoms are extremely uncomfortable, see a doctor.

An Injury to the Testicles, particularly during athletic events, is one of the most common and painful things that can happen to a male's sexual organs. By wearing an athletic supporter to protect and support your penis and testicles, you might prevent this from happening. Otherwise, the pain should go away fairly quickly. Sometimes, though, a testicle can actually twist around the cord from which it hangs, constricting the vessels that carry blood to the testicle. If the pain is quite severe and accompanied by nausea, vomiting, and fever, get to a doctor immediately. Surgery may be necessary.

Epididymitis is an inflammation of the tube that carries sperm from the testicle to the vas deferens, caused by bacteria from the urinary tract. The symptom of this condition is pain in the testicles. A doctor can take care of this problem with a prescription.

Retrograde Ejaculation is a fancy name for something that can be caused by an innocent action. Sometimes, when a male doesn't wish to ejaculate for some reason, he may put his hand or something over the penis during orgasm. If the semen doesn't come out the penis, it travels backward down the urethra and may be forced up the tube leading to the urethra. This could cause cloudy urine, discharge from the penis, and pain. The problem may clear up by itself, but it's best to see a doctor about these symptoms. He or she will treat the infection with medicine.

Undescended Testicles: Before you were born, your testicles were not in the scrotum, but up inside your body. Under normal circumstances, the testicles travel to the scrotum after birth. But sometimes one or both testicles don't descend, causing an undescended testicle. We don't know why this happens, but doctors can and do treat this condition, either with drugs or surgery. In a few cases, an undescended testicle is linked with cancer in this area. A regular testicular self-exam can help you find and get treatment for this cancer early (see "Cancer and the Testicular Self-Exam," page 81).

Swollen Glands: Even if you've never had sex, it's possible to get an infection in the lymph glands, located in your genitals. This is characterized by pain and swelling. A doctor can cure the problem with medicine.

Prostate Problems: The prostate gland, located at the base of the bladder, may become infected in younger men. This condition, called prostatitis, causes fever, pain when you have bowel movements, and pus in the urine. See a doctor for medicine if you experience these symptoms. Older men commonly have to see a doctor about an enlarged prostate gland, which decreases urinary flow and makes one feel an urgent need to urinate. Diet changes and sometimes surgery take care of the problem. The older a man gets, the more likely he is to develop prostate cancer, a disease that claims about 20,000 lives each year. A healthy diet, regular exercise, and frequent physical examinations help fight cancer (see Nutrition and Exercise).

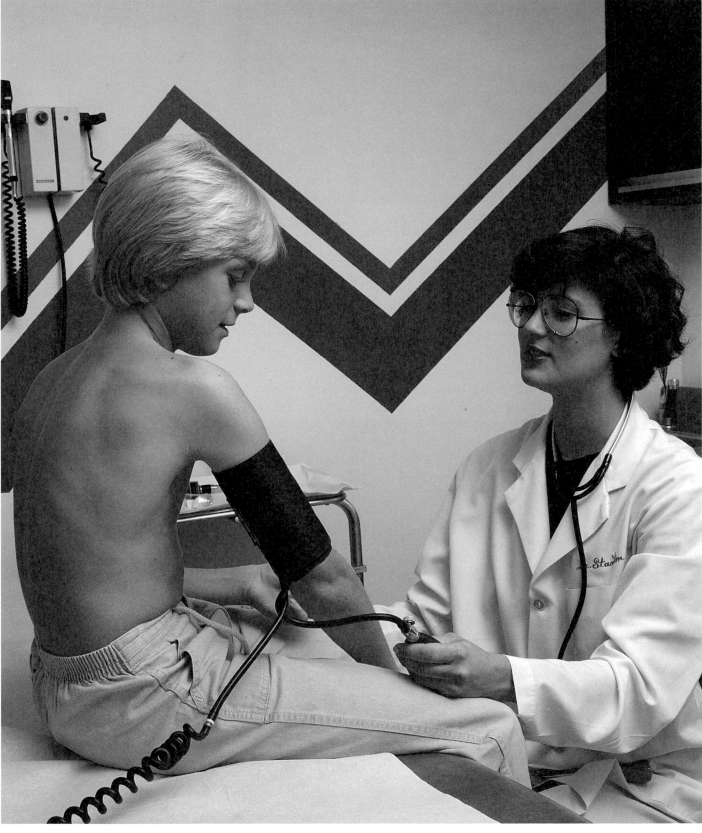

Did You Know...

Any unusal discharge or pain and burning upon urination should be checked out by a doctor? These could be signs of a sexually transmitted disease or an infection of the urethra.

Q. What is circumcision? Is there anything wrong with an uncircumcised penis?

A. When you're born, you have a loose piece of skin extending to the end of the penis called a "foreskin." Usually a doctor cuts this skin off a few days after the baby is born. This is called "circumcision," and it started out as a Jewish religious custom. Today most male babies are circumcised for hygienic reasons, though sometimes the foreskin sticks to the head of the penis and this procedure is necessary to get it unstuck. On occasion, the foreskin has such a small opening in it that the head of the penis can't be pushed through, and circumcision may be recommended. If your penis isn't circumcised, be sure to pull the foreskin back daily so it doesn't get too tight and so you can clean it thoroughly. Concentrate on the groove between the shaft and tip. Otherwise, a white, cheeselike substance called smegma forms behind the head of the penis, causing an unpleasant odor.

T F True or False?

If a boy has only one testicle, his production of sperm is reduced.

False. The body is great at adapting to things like this. Although most men are born with two testicles, sometimes a baby is born with one. Or an injury could crush a testicle so badly that it has to be removed. In this case the other testicle simply takes over and makes enough sperm necessary to impregnate a woman. A man's sex life is unaffected when a testicle is missing.

Cancer and the Testicular Self-Exam

Testicular cancer makes up fewer than one percent of all cancer cases, but nevertheless, it's a good idea to regularly check your testicles for any mysterious bumps or lumps. Although you're not in the high-risk age group (testicular cancer is one of the most common cancers in men aged twenty to thirty-five), this easy self-exam will enable you to seek help early in the unlikely event that something like this happens. It's a good idea to develop the habit of checking now. If you have undescended testicles or your testicles descended after the age of six, this exam is even more important, since you are forty times more likely to have this uncommon problem. After all, this exam takes only a few seconds and need only be performed once a month.

1. After a hot bath or shower, put your index and middle fingers on the underside of the scrotum, thumb on top.

2. Feel for a small lump about the size of a pea. This is your testicle. Roll it gently between your thumb and fingers.

3. Repeat this procedure with the other testicle.

4. Feel for the epididymis, a collection of coiled tubes at the back of the testicle.

What we've described here is what's *normal*. What could be abnormal? Any unusual lumps or bumps—soft or hard—toward the front or side of the testicle. If you think something feels funny, check with your mother or father, or a doctor. Though most unexplained bumps are not serious, it's always smart to be on the safe side.

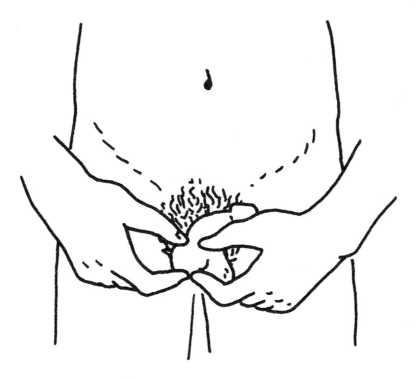

T_F True or False?

You can prevent the production of sperm by wearing tight underwear.

True and False. It's true that constricting the testicles or raising their temperature could hamper sperm production. But it's unlikely that you'll prevent a pregnancy by wearing tight underwear. However, tight clothes aren't healthy for your genitals.

Shaving

Maybe you're not at the point where it's time to shave yet, but you're probably looking forward to it. Because females don't grow distinctive facial hair like males (although they often do shave their legs and underarms), shaving seems like a very masculine routine.

Perhaps now all you need is a periodic trimming of your mustache, sideburns, and/or beard.

Eventually you may need to shave off your facial hair every day or even twice a day. Still other men just let their facial hair grow and rarely shave or trim. Of course, this is a matter of personal preference.

Once you do begin to shave, be sure your blade is new, sharp, and smooth. Your sister's or dad's razor may be dull, and thus more apt to cut and irritate your skin. To avoid this, you may prefer an electric razor. Some men don't like them, but it pays to try both and see for yourself.

Myths About Penis Size

1. Men with big thumbs have big penises.

2. Women enjoy sexual intercourse more when a man has a big penis.

3. Tall, large men have larger penises than short, small men.

4. Big penises make more sperm than small penises.

5. Very large penises won't fit into a woman's vagina.

Penis size has nothing to do with how big a man's body, nose, or anything else is. In fact, 90 percent of all men have erect penises measuring between five and seven inches (13–18 cm.). When it comes to sexual intercourse, the vagina is stretchable and can accommodate almost any size penis, except in very, very rare situations. Nor does penis size have anything to do with how much sperm the testicles make. Any feelings of inferiority you may have about your penis size should be reevaluated. Emotional closeness is more important for sexual satisfaction than penis size is.

Take the Level-Headed Approach to Sex

Perhaps you're not yet an adult, but nevertheless, you're beginning to deal with adult issues. One of them is sex. It would be easy to tell you to avoid thinking about sex for several years; the arguments against teenage sex, as you know, are convincing. But because you aren't a child any longer, you will have to make that decision on your own. Here's help:

Sex Lines to Watch Out For

Some time ago, newspaper columnist Ann Landers asked her readers to write in to tell her what people were saying to get unwilling partners to have sex. Here are some of the answers she got:

"If you really loved me you would. That's the way people express their true feelings. It's been going on since the world began."

"I promise we won't go all the way unless you want to. I'll stop whenever you say."

"It isn't sex I'm after. I'm really in love with you. If you get pregnant, I'll marry you."

"Life is so uncertain. Who knows whether you'll be alive tomorrow? It would be awful if you died in an accident or something without experiencing the greatest thrill of all."

"Come on. What are you afraid of? Don't be a baby. It's just part of growing up."

From "Sex and the Teenager," by Ann Landers, 1987

How to Say "No" to Sex

○ First of all, think hard about your feelings and values. If you truly believe that sex is to be shared by two people who've already become close in other ways, and if you recognize the risks of sex in young relationships, then it will be much easier to say "no."

○ If you're feeling pressured, tell your date this. Tell him or her that you're uncomfortable. Try to be simple and direct.

○ A good way to respond to "lines": "If you care enough to want to share sex with me, then you should care enough to understand why I don't want to do it. Stop trying to make me do something I don't want to do."

○ Don't lead your date on. By saying things that suggest you might be interested in sex, your date may feel that *you* are the one expecting sex.

○ Don't get trapped. If your boyfriend or girlfriend is under the influence of drugs or alcohol, or if he or she is sexually aggressive, then avoid being alone with your date.

*Remember: If saying "no" to sex means the relationship is over, then that relationship isn't very strong to begin with.

Reasons Why Some Teens Don't Wait to Have Sex

GIRLS:
1. Peer pressure

2. Boys talk girls into it

3. Everyone is doing it

4. Curiosity

5. In love with partner

6. Want to feel grown up

BOYS:
1. Peer pressure

2. Curiosity

3. Everyone is doing it

4. Want sexual gratification

5. (tie) Friends talk about it

   Makes you feel cool

   Want to feel grown up

© Edward Lettau/FPG International

From "American Teens Speak: Sex, Myths, TV, and Birth Control," The Planned Parenthood Poll, 1986.

Where Sex Attitudes Come From

Values vary from person to person, and it might take some real soul-searching to figure out how you really feel. For example, deep down, you probably feel a certain way about sex. Maybe you genuinely believe that teenage sex is fine. Or maybe you feel really guilty about just *kissing,* let alone having sexual intercourse. Both of these are values. Aside from sex, if you feel that having a family and a good job are important, those are values, too.

In any case, it's easy to get caught up in what "everybody else thinks." However you feel is a reflection on you. How do we arrive at these values? Some come from religious beliefs; some from television shows you watch, music you hear, and books you read. And of course, family, friends, and teachers influence you as well.

In the next few years you'll have to make some decisions about sex. But before you decide, think about your values and where they come from. You might be surprised by some of your own opinions.

Q. *How far is too far?*

A. What you really mean is: When I'm on a date or with my girlfriend or boyfriend, where should I draw the line?''

That's a question that only you can answer. But if you need some guidelines, consider this: First of all, you know the arguments against having sexual intercourse until you are an adult involved in a long-term relationship. Pregnancy, sexually transmitted diseases, and emotional commitments, among other things, can stay with you long after the actual sexual act. How about touching each other's genitals? It won't lead to STD's or pregnancy, but most people have a difficult time stopping right there. Sexual desire being what it is, most people don't stop.

Now, you look at all these factors and make an informed decision as to how far is too far.

© Steve Smith/Wheeler Pictures

An STD Glossary

Sexually transmitted, or venereal, diseases are some of the most threatening infectious diseases of our time. One in every fifty teenagers gets gonorrhea, and as many as half of all young people may contract an STD by the age of twenty-five.

Most STD's are passed on by genital contact. Other victims get their disease at birth, from infected mothers. One STD may do little but prompt warts on your genitals; others can kill you. Avoiding an STD is relatively easy, a lot easier than treating it. And it doesn't help that some of these diseases can be present without symptom. Here are more facts:

Acquired Immune Deficiency Syndrome (AIDS)

Symptoms: Extreme tiredness, persistent fever, weight loss, painful lymph nodes, growths or sores on the skin, diarrhea, unexplained bleeding

Symptoms usually appear: Six months to five years after infection, but doctors aren't sure

How it's passed on: Through close contact with bodily fluids, usually blood or semen of the infected person (through sexual intercourse, blood transfusions, infected hypodermic needles, birth, or in some cases, infected blood coming in contact with an open wound, your eyes, or mouth).

Treatment: As of now, none that are totally effective.

Complications: Fatal, about half of all AIDS victims die within a year of diagnosis 75 to 80 percent within two years

Note: Teenagers account for less than one percent of all AIDS cases.

Chlamydia

Symptoms: Burning sensation during urination or vaginal or urethral discharge; often occurs along with other STD's, although there may be no symptoms.

How it's passed on: Sexual intercourse with an infected partner

Treatment: Medication or perhaps surgery.

Complications: For men, inability to produce sperm; for women, pelvic inflammatory disease (see Q&A, page 90) or inability to get pregnant

Note: Public health officials fear that chlamydia, a disease that infects 2.5 to 3 million Americans, may be even more common than estimated—and spreading.

Gonorrhea (also called: dose, clap, drip)

Symptoms: Sometimes there are no symptoms, but when there are, they may include white or yellowish discharge from genitals or anus, pain during bowel movements, and throat infections. Also, women may experience a dull pain in the lower abdomen after menstruation.

Symptoms usually appear: Within two to nine days, but up to thirty days after infection.

How it's passed on: By direct contact of one person's genitals, mouth, or nose with another person's genitals, mouth, or nose.

Treatment: Medicine

Complications: A blood infection that can spread to the heart or nervous system; swollen joints resulting from arthritis; and in women, pelvic inflammatory disease. Men may also have erection problems.

Note: Men usually know they have this disease because it is very painful for them. Nine out of ten women, however, have no symptoms at all. It is estimated that 5 percent of sexually active American women have gonorrhea and are unaware of it.

Herpes II (usually called herpes)

Symptoms: Painful blisters on the genitals, pubic area, buttocks, or thighs; painful urination; swollen glands; fever.

Symptoms usually appear: At different times

How it's passed on: Direct contact of mouth or genitals with blisters or open sores caused by herpes virus.

Treatment: No cure, but for relief of the painful sores, doctors recommend compresses, cleanliness, and sometimes medicines. There is now a medication that can help to prevent the flairup of herpes.

Complications: Herpes may be linked with cervical cancer in women.

Note: Even after herpes sores clear up, they can return without warning days or years later. Active sores infect sexual partners and babies at birth. Babies can die from herpes.

Pediculosis Pubis (also called crabs, cooties)

Symptoms: Intense itching, tiny blood spots on underpants, lice in pubic hair

Symptoms usually appear: One to four weeks after infection.

How it's passed on: By direct contact with the infested area, or from lice on beds or clothes

Treatment: Medicine; thorough cleaning

Complications: Infections from scratching. Also, this disorder is frequently accompanied by other STD's.

Syphilis (also called: syph, pox, bad blood)

Symptoms: Stage 1 is characterized by a dime-sized, open lump or crater-like sore at the place where the bacteria entered the body, such as the mouth, throat, vagina, rectum, or penis. This sore, or chancre (pronounced shank-er), usually appears three to four weeks after infection, but can appear as soon as ten but as long as ninety days later.

During Stage 2, anywhere from one to twelve months after the chancre's appearance, these symptoms may or may not appear: rashes on moist parts of the skin; white patches on the

mouth or throat; temporary baldness; sore throat; swollen glands; pain in the joints. Symptoms may last up to two years.

How it's passed on: Direct contact with the sores, rashes, or patches in the mouth or genitals

Treatment: Medicine

Complications: If untreated after several years, can lead to brain damage, blindness, insanity, paralysis, heart disease, perhaps death; also damage to newborn babies

Note: Once inside the body, the bacteria that causes syphilis mimics the symptoms of many major diseases.

Trichomoniasis (also called: tric, vaginitis)

Symptoms: In women, a heavy, frothy discharge, intense burning, itching, and redness of the genitals. Men may have a slight, clear discharge and itching after urination, but they usually experience no symptoms.

Symptoms usually appear: One to four weeks after infection

How it's passed on: Direct contact with infectious area

Treatment: Medicine

Complications: Gland soreness and swelling

Venereal Warts

Symptoms: Wartlike growths on the genitals or anus; itching; irritation

Symptoms usually appear: One to three months after infection

How it's passed on: Direct contact with warts

Treatment: No cure, but warts can be removed by medicine or surgery

Complications: Very contagious, and can spread enough to block openings of the vagina, rectum, and throat; also, may be linked to cervical cancer in women

When It's Time to See a Doctor

There are other less common STD's and genital disorders not mentioned here. If you are sexually active and do have any of the following symptoms, you should see a doctor:

Painful burning during urination

Dark-colored urine

Discharges from the penis or vagina that itch, burn, or have an unusual odor

Persistent sore throat

Soreness, redness, sores, warts, or an unexplained pimple in the genital area

Q. What is pelvic inflammatory disease?

A. PID occurs when infection starts at the vagina, moves to the cervix, uterus, fallopian tubes, and eventually, out of the open tubes and into the pelvic cavity. PID can be caused by many different types of bacteria but is primarily associated with gonorrhea. In fact, among American women who have had gonorrhea, 10 to 17 percent end up with this serious disorder. Doctors are still studying other causes. The initial symptoms of PID include pelvic pain, chills, fever, irregular menstrual periods, and lower back pain, but complications include constant pain in the pelvic region, pain during sexual intercourse, abnormal pregnancies, and even sterility—the inability to have babies. PID has been known to cause sterility in up to 18,000 girls between the ages of fifteen and nineteen.

© Zehr/FPG International

Pay attention to your body. Some of the "out of sync" feelings you have may be perfectly normal. But whenever you have doubts or your family and friends express concern about you—it's wise to check with a doctor. His or her job is to help you understand what's going on in your body.

D*id You Know . . .*

That using a condom can give both sexual partners protection against STDs? But remember: Sores not covered by a condom can still transmit infection skin to skin.

Other birth-control devices, the diaphragm and vaginal contraceptives (see "Birth Control," pages 93–95), offer some, but not as much protection and only to females. Interestingly, urinating and washing genitals thoroughly with soap and water immediately after intercourse can lessen the risk of infection, especially when it comes to syphilis.

T **F** *True or False?*

A person who does not have sex does not have to worry about STD's.

True! Except for pediculosis pubis, which can be transmitted by an infected person's bedsheets or clothes, STD's are passed by direct contact. This means you have to touch an infected person's genitals or sores. Of course, you'll want to look out for sores or growths on the mouth or throat of your partner before you kiss.

Birth Control

You've read about how an unplanned pregnancy can cause problems for uncommitted adults—and of course, teenagers, too. But how do people prevent pregnancy when they have intercourse?

The only birth-control measure that is 100 percent sure is avoiding sexual intercourse. But some measures are almost as effective; the others are certainly better than no birth control at all. Some of these methods have to be prescribed by a doctor or can be obtained from certain agencies (see "Where to Get Help," page 111). Other methods can be bought over-the-counter at the drug-store. How do people choose the best method? It all depends on people's needs and preferences. Here's what they can consider:

The Pill is just that—a Pill that is taken by a woman every day on a monthly cycle. By releasing certain hormones in the body, the Pill keeps the ovaries from releasing eggs, and thus, prevents pregnancy. How well does the Pill work? If 100 women were to take the pill as directed for a year, only about two might get pregnant. This is usually because they forget to take the pill for a day or more. The advantages: The Pill results in

fewer pregnancies than any other birth-control measure, plus it's the easiest. The Pill has been linked to blood clots, stroke, heart attack, or liver tumors, but these risks are very, very small for women under 35 who do not smoke. A woman has to see a doctor for an examination before she can get a prescription for the Pill.

For a while, the **condom** was losing in popularity to other birth-control measures, but since doctors have been recommending its use to fight against sexually transmitted diseases (especially AIDS), it is once again very much in demand. What is it? A condom is a balloon-shaped sheath of thin rubber

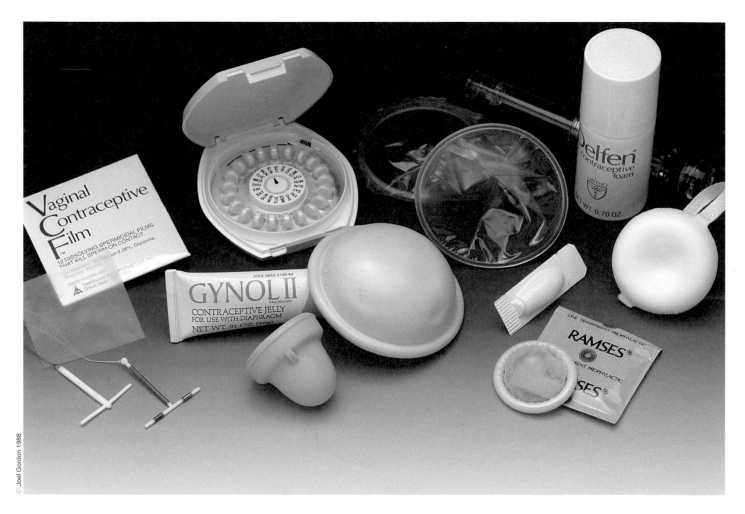

© Joel Gordon 1988

Contraceptives, clockwise from left top corner: Vaginal Contraceptive Film is a form of spermicide; The Pill; a Vaginal Condom, a newer form of birth control not yet approved by the Food and Drug Administration; Vaginal Foam; a Vaginal Sponge, another form of spermicide; a Condom; a Spermicidal Suppository; a Diaphragm and Spermicidal Jelly; a Cervical Cap; two Intrauterine Devices (IUDs).

or animal tissue, placed on a man's erect penis before intercourse. During orgasm, the condom collects a man's semen and keeps it from entering a woman's vagina. The condom is 90 percent effective for prevention of pregnancy when used alone, but the odds are even better when a condom is used along with a vaginal chemical contraceptive. For the best results, it's important for sexual partners to use the condom correctly: When it's rolled over the erect penis, a space of about one-half inch (1 cm.) should be left at the tip to catch the semen. After the orgasm but before the erection subsides, the man should hold the rim of the condom against the penis as he withdraws from the vagina. This way, the condom can't slip and spill the semen. The final step: Throw away the condom. Condoms (and vaginal chemical contraceptives) can be purchased by anyone, no matter what age.

Vaginal chemical contraceptives or spermicides are foams, creams, jellies, and suppositories (a substance pushed in with fingers) that are inserted deep into the vagina before intercourse. These contraceptives spread over the entrance to the uterus, blocking and/or killing sperm. Alone, these birth-control measures aren't as effective as the Pill: Out of 100 women using one of these products, 18 may get pregnant during the first year. However, doctors now say one of the best contraceptives is the condom-spermicide team. The only real complaints heard about these products are that some people think they're messy and a woman or man may experience a slight genital irritation. Like the condom, spermicides can be bought at the drugstore.

Many women choose the **diaphragm** because it has no side effects and has reasonably good results, especially if it's used exactly as recommended. This soft, rubber, saucer-shaped cup is covered with a special cream or jelly, then inserted in the woman's vagina (almost like a tampon) before intercourse. Some women either forget to put it in or don't get it in quite right, so the diaphragm has·a 19 percent failure rate. In order to get the right size diaphragm and learn how to insert it, women go to the doctor for this birth-control measure.

One of the newer forms of birth control is the **cervical cap**. In fact, the United States approved its use as recently as May 1988. The cap is a flexible, cuplike device—about 1½ inches (3.5 centimeters) in diameter—that fits on the base of the cervix to block the passage of sperm. Like the diaphragm, it is used with spermicide. Unlike the diaphragm, the cap is smaller, and for some women, more comfortable. The cervical cap is available only by prescription. Once a patient is fitted by a doctor, she inserts and removes the cap herself. Studies show the cap is about 85 percent effective in preventing pregnancy.

Although it was once fairly popular, the **intrauterine device** (IUD) is almost non-existent now. Not only are the possible problems linked with the IUD numerous, a few women have had serious infections stemming from its use. That's why all manufacturers but one have stopped making IUD's. How it works: A plastic device is inserted by a doctor in the uterus. Somehow, though doctors aren't sure exactly how, the IUD acts to change the lining of the uterus to keep a pregnancy from happening. Of 100 women with IUD's, about 5 may become pregnant during the first year of actual use. Couples are often attracted to the IUD because it doesn't require planning or remembering, such as taking a pill every day or insertion of the diaphragm for every sex act. But the side effects range from bleeding during periods to pelvic infections.

The **rhythm method** is the most unsuccessful form of birth control, with a failure rate of 24 percent. To practice the rhythm method, a couple has to plan very carefully and study the female's body functions for months. By doing this, they try to predict when ovulation occurs, and therefore when to avoid sexual intercourse. As you might guess, this isn't easy to do, since menstrual cycles vary from month to month. Plus, this birth-control method is a lot of trouble; doctors say the woman involved has to take her temperature every day and check her vaginal secretions. Even though the rhythm method is attractive in that it has no bodily side effects and requires no medication and little equipment, doctors rarely recommend the rhythm method.

Reasons Why Teenagers Don't Use Contraceptives During Sexual Intercourse

GIRLS:

1. No need, pregnancy won't happen to them

2. Unexpected sex, therefore no time

3. Don't know enough about them

4. Afraid parents will find out

BOYS:

1. Don't know enough about them

2. Unexpected sex, no time

3. No need, pregnancy won't happen to their girlfriends

From "American Teens Speak: Sex, Myths, TV, and Birth Control," The Planned Parenthood Poll, 1986.

What About Abortion?

Abortion isn't the prevention of a pregnancy, but the ending of one by surgery. A few different methods are used today, but the most common one is called "vacuum aspiration." Essentially, the doctor removes the fertilized egg from the female's uterus with a hollow suction tube. The operation takes between five and ten minutes.

Today, abortion is relatively risk-free, physically speaking, even more so than carrying a pregnancy full-term. However, if abortion is performed by an unqualified person or particularly by a pregnant woman herself, the danger factor is very high. Although abortion is legal when it's performed by a doctor, before 1973 it was illegal by any means. The result was that many women got sick and died from having abortions done under far-less-than-safe conditions.

Why do people want abortions? Because they do not wish to be pregnant. Many young, unmarried women look to abortion because having a child would cause many problems for them. But sometimes married women have reasons for not wanting pregnancy, such as a career or too many other children at home. Occasionally doctors recommend abortion when pregnancy will risk the mother's life, for medical reasons, or when it's discovered early that the unborn baby is severely handicapped. Finally, women who become pregnant when they were raped or coerced into sex sometimes turn to abortion.

Like any important issue, there are good arguments both for and against abortion. Many teenagers consider abortion when they accidentally get pregnant; it saves them from life-long decisions about marriage, single motherhood, and giving the baby up for adoption. Few people disagree that a raped woman should have the right to an abortion.

But in most cases, abortion is a difficult choice to make. While some people are very insistent about a person's right to legal abortions, other people are very much opposed to abortion in any case. Those arguments are good, too. They question: At which point is the fertilized egg a fetus (unborn baby)?; Who is entitled to say that a fetus doesn't have the right to live? Religious groups are concerned that we are "making God's decisions"—that babies at any stage of the pregnancy are meant to be.

The moral considerations involved in making judgments about abortion are very complex. Some people who oppose abortion don't recognize that many unwanted babies are born today into difficult and sad circumstances. Unwanted pregnancies also complicate a lot of unmarried parents' lives; you already know some of the statistics. In fact, teenage pregnancies are more likely to result in medical problems for the mother and child.

But on the other hand, there is concern that abortion is overused, that people view it as birth control and not surgery. This moral issue could be avoided by the use of contraceptives or, in some cases, the avoidance of sex altogether.

Abortion is one of the most emotionally charged issues of this decade. But no matter what your personal opinion is, women considering abortion need support and wise counseling.

Options for Pregnant Teens

○ Abortion

○ Having the baby and giving it up for adoption

○ Having the baby and becoming a single mother

○ Having the baby and independently sharing care of the baby, without marriage

○ Marriage

Q. Does douching prevent pregnancy?

A. Douching is a way of cleaning the vagina by flushing it out with a water-and-vinegar solution or with packaged products. A special squeezable plastic bottle or hot-water bottle is used to squirt the liquid in the vagina, and the liquid is allowed to drain back out.

Not only do most doctors disapprove of douching for cleansing the vagina, they know for a fact that it doesn't prevent pregnancy. Sperm can move so rapidly, the douche is not likely to wash them out of the vagina in time. In some cases, the fluid may actually help the sperm move upward into the cervical canal.

Doctors generally don't recommend douching for hygiene purposes because it could cause an imbalance of healthy bacteria in the vagina. This bacteria helps prevent vaginal infections. Plus, the vagina secretes its own fluids to naturally wash away impurities, so douching probably isn't necessary.

Note: Even though the vagina has its own cleansing system, it's still important to regularly wash the genitals. Perspiration and other secretions can cause them to have an unpleasant odor.

How Can a Woman Tell If She's Pregnant?

First of all, if the woman hasn't participated in sexual activity that would allow sperm to enter the vagina, there's no reason for her to suspect that she's pregnant. However, if she has been sexually active in this manner—and especially if she hasn't been using contraceptives—she should look out for these signs:

- One or two missed periods (the most reliable sign)
- Nausea (a need to vomit)
- Swollen, tender breasts
- Increased vaginal secretions
- Fatigue (feeling extremely tired)
- Constipation or diarrhea
- Frequent urination

Any female who suspects she's pregnant should see a doctor, or visit Planned Parenthood or a similar gynecological clinic for a pregnancy test. If the pregnancy is unwanted, an expert can help her decide how to handle it. If the pregnancy is wanted, then regular physical examinations are necessary to make sure the baby remains healthy (see also "Where to Get Help," page 111).

T_F True or False?

Sex is a good experience.

True and False. Sex is good for some of the people, some of the time. However, even married people who are very much in love will tell you that day-to-day life interferes with sex. Because sex is as much a mental act as it is physical, a number of things can make it less than satisfactory: a bad day at work, lack of privacy, feeling tired, and differences of opinion about when to have sex can make a difference in how "good" it is. No matter what television, magazines, and books lead us to believe, sex is no magical mystery, even if it is an important part of a mature relationship.

There's something else you should know. The first time is usually *not* "a good experience." Frequently, the male is nervous about his performance, making it difficult to get and keep an erection. If the female has an intact (not broken or stretched) hymen, she may feel some pain when a penis enters her vagina. And of course, apprehension also affects her enjoyment. In fact, females rarely have an orgasm the first time they have intercourse. For males, ejaculation signifies orgasm, and some boys can ejaculate in spite of nervousness.

© Billy G. Barnes/FPG International

Sexual Abuse: A Sore Subject

What is sexual abuse and what is acceptable sexual behavior? Lawyers can argue all day about where the line should be drawn. Still, you're old enough to know when you're asked or forced to do something that's wrong or that you don't want to do. Examples:

○ Sexual intercourse against your will
○ Being asked to look at or touch someone's penis or vagina
○ Being asked to let someone touch your breasts, vagina, penis, or buttocks
○ Being asked to look at nude photos
○ Being asked to pose naked for photographs
○ Being asked to undress so someone can see you nude

You're the best judge about what constitutes sexual abuse. If your boyfriend or girlfriend asks you to have sexual intercourse, that's different than *forcing* you to have sexual intercourse. However, if an adult—say, your mother's friend—asks you to have sexual intercourse, something is definitely wrong.

Different sorts of sexual abuse have varying characteristics. *Rape* may refer to any forced sex act, but it's most often used to describe sexual intercourse with a female by a male without her consent. People assume that rape is frequently committed by a stranger, but information from the Department of Justice says in fact, most victims actually know their attackers. Sometimes called "date rape," this is a big problem for girls between thirteen and eighteen. Reasons:

1. Girls and boys this age don't always recognize what constitutes rape. Many boys think it's okay to force a date to let him touch or have sex with her. Similarly, girls aren't clear on what a male can and cannot do before he violates her rights.

2. Guilt gets in the way of stopping or reporting forced sex. Example: If a girl invites a boy over when her parents are gone, she may say nothing about a forced sexual act because she is afraid her parents will be angry with her. Or a girl may ask "What did I do to deserve it? It must have been something I said or did."

3. Girls may "cover up" a forced sex act because they want to "keep" their boyfriends.

4. A young woman's embarrassment may stop her from asking questions before a forced sex act or from reporting it afterwards. Questions like: "Will your parents be at home?" or "Don't you think we've gone far enough?" Often females fear physical examinations and police questioning, damage to their reputations, or further abuse. Sometimes they want to protect their attackers because they know them.

Date rape is not solely a female concern. Many males report being coerced into sex by women when they really did not want to. The most important thing to remember is that you never lose the right to say, "Stop. I don't want to go any further." Never accept the blame for being forced to do something you didn't want to do and tried to stop. No one has the right to do that.

There are plenty of cases in which girls are raped by strangers. But steps can be taken to lower the risk of these crimes happening to girls *or* boys (see below). Other terms to know:

Statutory rape is a legal term describing sexual intercourse between an adult and an under-age girl or sometimes a boy. It doesn't matter if the young person agrees to have sex or not; if a thirteen-year-old girl has sex with a twenty-three-year-old man, he could be in trouble legally. The law assumes the adult is responsible.

Incest is perhaps the most devastating form of sexual abuse, because it involves two members of

the same family—who are too close to be legally married—being sexual, whether it is touching and feeling or sexual intercourse. Incest is such a taboo subject that the victim is even less likely than other abuse victims to tell anyone what is happening, since it could result in break-up of the family, prison for the offender, or rejection of the victim by the rest of the family. Even so, incest is far more common than most people realize; in 1982 alone, the American Humane Association had 48,000 reported cases (with some cases unreported). Stepfamilies, fathers and daughters, uncles and nieces, and brothers and sisters are the most common relationships in which incest occurs, but incest involving other relatives and homosexual relationships are not unheard of.

Sexual abuse also includes *child molesting*, known as pedophilia. Whether a person is six or sixteen, one thing is clear: No one has the right to touch your body without your consent.

Read on for tips that may help you avoid circumstances that could lead to sexual abuse. If you have ever been sexually abused and have feelings or thoughts that still bother you, professional counseling may help (see "What to Do When You Have Been Sexually Abused," page 106).

More and more, you'll see public service announcements like this in newspapers and other publications. The public is more aware of child abuse than it once was.

True or False?

Boys cannot be raped.

False. Now, it *is* true that most rape victims are females and most rapists are males. Yet it is possible for a woman to use a weapon or guilt to force a man to have sex with her. It's also possible for a man to be raped by another man. Males have also been victim to incest, either by a female or another male. So even though most rape and incest information seems to be written for females, boys who have been victimized by sexual abuse should take the same steps. Call the police, hospital, or a rape hotline (see "What to Do When You Have Been Sexually Abused," page 106).

True or False?

Incest is only incest when the victim has been forced to have sexual relations with someone else.

False. Because incest is a crime generally committed by an older family member, the younger victim is easily influenced to do things he or she doesn't want to do—from kissing and petting to actual intercourse. Even if the incest victim thinks it's wrong, he or she may keep quiet because of feelings of confusion or not wanting to get in trouble or cause a family problem. Family members have been known to take the side of the incest offender in blaming the incest victim. The offender may also convince the victim that he or she caused the sexual abuse.

Whatever the circumstances, however, it's very important for a victim to get help and protection. Likewise, people who commit incest and other sexual crimes are in need of help.

Preventing Rape

○ Don't let a date you don't know well take you to an isolated spot, such as a park, empty parking lot, or wooded area.

○ Don't always give a date the benefit of the doubt. Even the best of boyfriends—the classiest, the most educated, the most affluent, the most famous—could be a disturbed individual who will force sex on an unwilling victim.

○ Don't let anyone into your home without making sure of his identity. Attackers sometimes pose as deliverymen, meter readers, repairmen, and so on.

○ Don't get on an elevator with a suspicious-looking person. If you find yourself on an elevator with a suspicious person, stand near the buttons. In an emergency, push as many buttons as you can, including the alarm.

○ Always have your keys ready when you're opening the door to your car or home.

○ At night, walk on well-lighted sidewalks and streets. At any time, avoid deserted streets, shortcuts, parks, and parking lots.

○ Don't hitchhike.

○ Always be aware of your surroundings: people who might be following you, doorways where someone can hide, cars that pull up behind you.

○ If you're being followed, ring the nearest doorbell.

○ Scream and run if you have to.

If You are Attacked

If you are attacked, there are different ways you can react. As nervous as you might be, you should try to think what the best response is. Maybe you'll try one of the following, and if that doesn't work, you'll do something else.

1. Stall for time. Try to talk your attacker out of doing anything he might regret. Even if you can't convince him, someone might come along in the meantime.

2. Turn off your attacker by sticking your fingers down your throat and vomiting or urinating. Or tell him you have AIDS or syphylis or that you're an IV drug-user.

3. Tell him that you brother, father, or some other male will be home any moment, come by to pick you up, or be looking for you.

4. Scream "fire" instead of "police," since people often avoid getting involved in crimes. Pull a fire alarm box if it's nearby.

5. Make any noise you can; yell, break windows, bang on walls, etc. Someone may respond.

6. Fight back, if your attacker isn't armed with weapons. Kick your attacker in the groin, stomp on his foot, jab your thumbs in his eyes, use your key and aim for his eyes, temples, ears, or Adam's apple.

7. However, if you think you might get hurt by defending yourself, or if everything else fails, then it might be best to submit. This is better than getting killed or seriously injured. Even if you don't fight back, the act is still rape. Follow the steps listed below.

What to Do When You Have Been Sexually Abused

1. Call the police. They'll get a report and take you to the hospital for a medical examination. (Many victims have difficulty in deciding whether to report a rape, especially when the rapist is a friend or acquaintance. If this is the case, see number 2.)

2. Call a rape crisis center or rape hotline, listed under "Rape" or "Community Services" in the yellow pages. They'll help you get to the hospital and decide whether to file a police report. A Planned Parenthood center will also have the information needed to help a young person through the medical exam, and if desired, a police report.

3. Get a medical examination. If you call the police or your local rape crisis center, they'll help you take care of this first. If you wish to make your own arrangements, all you have to do is go to a hospital emergency room. Whether or not the rape is reported to the police, an exam is necessary to determine whether there have been injuries, test for STD's or pregnancy, and provide the medical evidence necessary to prosecute. It's important that you *not* shower or bathe before the test.

4. If you aren't able or don't wish to take these steps on your own, talk to an adult about it. When incest or child abuse is the problem, it's usually best to go outside the immediate family for help (teachers, neighbors, friends' parents, minister, priest, grandparents, aunts, or uncles). When members of the family are guilty of sexual crimes, parents sometimes have trouble dealing with the truth. Even so, it's important to report sexual abuse. It's a crime no one has the right to commit.

Seek Support

Do you have any questions so far? Of course you do, and you have plenty of answers yet to find. And no wonder: Sex is complex, so it's not completely understood by adults, much less by someone who's just being introduced to it.

Not that you should think about sex as a big mystery. You've read already that sex is very important, but it has its practical, everyday side. It's perfectly understandable that you have lots of questions about sex and how you are changing. At the same time, you should realize that you're not alone in this. If you feel a little overwhelmed at the way time is leaping ahead of you, take a look around. You'll see a whole classroom of people who are experiencing the same thing. What's more, there are plenty of people who've already been through what you're going through, so ideally, they'll understand what it feels like.

In Stress and Mental Health, we emphasized how important it is to *talk* out your problems. Holding in all your insecurities and questions will only cause more problems. A topic like human sexuality—even if it isn't the most widely accepted conversation-starter—shouldn't be held back, either. Look for answers, and you'll know what to expect and how to best deal with sex and hormonal changes. Lean on a shoulder, and you'll be able to get through the toughest times with ease. Don't forget to listen and lend your own shoulder to confused friends and parents, too. You'll help someone else, plus you'll feel better about turning to them for support later.

Where should you turn for this kind of support? First, your parents. Many teens feel most comfortable asking Mom about menstruation or Dad about shaving, and why not? They've always been there for you, and they have experienced puberty themselves. What's more, parents have personal stock in you, so they're more apt to be interested in your problems and needs. Parents are also the best source for predictions. Because you're likely to follow in his footsteps, Dad can tell you when *his* voice first began to change, and when yours might, too.

But remember: Parents are people, too. While some may be very open about sex, others won't discuss it all. You probably already know how your parents feel about sex. If they've always answered your questions honestly and explained birth control, STD's, and other issues, then you probably feel free to go to them. On the other hand, if Mom never talked to you about menstruation, and sex is a taboo subject in your house, you probably feel a little apprehensive about questioning her. Most parents are in-between these extremes: They'll answer your questions as best they can, but they're still embarrassed. It has a lot to do with the way society has been so hush-hush about sex in the past. More and more, people are bringing important questions into the open, but it's taking time. Your parents may not be quite used to it yet.

Scores of advice books have been written for parents who don't know how to talk to their children about sexuality, but if you have unanswered questions, or if you sense that your parents don't know how to approach the subject, there's nothing to stop you from going to them. Be honest. Say, "Mom, this is hard for me to talk about, but I'm worried about how the other eighth-grade boys are ahead of me—physically." Chances are, Mom will appreciate your honesty.

Some parents will warm up to your curiosity and tell you what they can. Some will try, but may be unable to answer your questions or talk candidly. (Don't be quick to blame them; maybe their own parents were this way and they simply cannot change.) Then there are parents who will express anger at your interest in sexuality. They might accuse you of thinking too much about it or even performing sexual acts.

It's too bad if this happens, because studies show that *informed* teens, who understand and feel comfortable about sexuality, are least likely to have problems with pregnancy, STD's, and other pre-marital sex problems. Yet teens frequently find themselves up against a brick wall when it comes to getting answers from parents. If that's the case, you have to go outside the home. Friends are always a good sounding block. You probably enjoy "comparing notes" about sex and growing up, though you'll probably find that peers your own age may be just as confused as you are.

Talk to your friends about what is happening to you. They're probably going through the same thing, which will make you feel better.

Even though some of them may actually know about sex, they can also be the source of wrong information. In fact, fellow teens are often the source of sexual myths, such as "You can't get pregnant if you stand up while having sex," or

"Gay people try to convert straight people into living their way."

Seek out your friends for support, but for facts, talk to your parents or the professionals listed under "Where to Get Help" (page 111).

uiz: Parents and Sex

On your own paper, write down the answers to these questions. Then read on to see how you compare with other teenagers in the United States.

1. Have either of your parents ever talked with you about sex and how pregnancy is caused?

2. How old were you when they first talked to you about this?

3. Have your parents or any other adult in your family *ever* talked with you about using birth control methods?

4. Do you think that you would be nervous or afraid to bring up the subject of sex and birth control with your parents?

According to a recent Planned Parenthood Poll of 1,000 teens, most parents (about 70 percent) did talk to them about sex. But only one-third of the teens had discussed birth control with their parents. Another one-third had not heard anything from their parents on this matter.

About half of the young people were nervous or afraid to bring up the subject. Among the kids who had already talked to their parents about sex and pregnancy, most of them were under thirteen when the subject was discussed.

*From "American Teens Speak: Sex, Myths, TV, and Birth Control," The Planned Parenthood Poll, 1986.

Where to Get Help

Here are a number of sources for help or advice about issues of sexuality.

Your Doctor

Don't feel funny about asking your doctor questions. It's his or her job to answer them. But maybe you have a doctor who tends to brush you off. Or maybe she or he won't give you information because you're "too young." Or perhaps you're afraid your doctor will tell your parents things you don't want them to be told. Under these circumstances, it might be wise to find your *own* doctor who will respect your wishes. Or visit a family planning clinic.

Family Planning Clinics

Organizations like Planned Parenthood will not only dispense information about birth control and STD's, some also have special groups and classes for teenagers on these topics. You can probably find the local branch of Planned Parenthood in your phone directory's white pages. Call and set up an appointment to talk to a counselor, or just ask about any programs they may have for teenagers. You can also look under "family planning information" or "birth control information" in the yellow pages for similar organizations. Sometimes information and services are free. Ask.

Other Organizations

The local YWCA, YMCA, community hotline, health-care clinic, or women's center might also be able to put you in touch with a teen group or other services for young people interested in finding out more about sex and hormonal changes.

One problem you might encounter is that some groups falsely advertise to teens to trick them into coming in for help. They may have a name that makes you think they're interested in helping you, but once you make an appointment, you'll find that their motives are to teach their own values and beliefs. It could be that they're advocating abortion *or* they're against it.

It's probably best to avoid these organizations, since you should be making your own informed decisions as to what to do with your life. Before you make an appointment, call and ask for the group's philosophy. Ask questions and see if a reference can be provided: a doctor or patient you can trust. If you decide to make an appointment, have someone come with you. These organizations are less likely to use guilt or other tactics to persuade you to their point of view if you are not alone. Don't forget to ask about confidentiality, too. Unless you're in an emergency situation, you're always entitled to privacy.

Other Adults

Some areas of the country may not have the special services mentioned above. It doesn't hurt to find out first, since these organizations are organized to help you *and* obligated to keep your personal information private. But if you're unsuccessful in locating the right place to go for answers and you're unable to talk to your parents, talk to your favorite teacher, your best friend's mother, a guidance counselor at school, an older brother or sister, or anyone you trust. While there's no denying you're a mature person who's responsible for your own actions, it's also true that adults usually have more experience in these matters. Not only will it help *you* to talk about your questions, an adult might also be able to point you in the right direction.

Quiz: Sex Ed at School

On your own paper, write the answers to the following questions. Then read on to find out how your school compares with some others in the United States.

1. Have you had a formal class or course in sex education at school?

2. If so, did it include biological facts about reproduction?

3. Did it include talk about coping with your sexual development?

4. Did it include information about different kinds of birth control?

5. Did it include information about preventing sexual abuse?

6. Did it include facts about abortion?

7. Did it include facts about where to get contraceptives?

According to a recent Planned Parenthood poll, four out of ten American teenagers have not had sex ed at school. Among the students who have, two-thirds did not get what experts consider a good background in sexual education. To have this kind of comprehensive study, your school would need to teach you about four of the six topics in Questions 2–7, above. Almost 90 percent of the schools with sex ed told their students about reproduction, but only 50 percent or so provided information on contraceptives, abortion, and sexual abuse.

Why is sex education important? Because research shows that education helps teens deal with sex and hormonal changes. Since students say that sex education is their third most important source of information (behind parents and friends), informed teens are less likely to have problems with premature pregnancy and STD's.

You can see, then, why teens need parents and sex education classes to help them. If your school is lacking a good sex ed program, it might be wise to talk to your parents and teachers. With their help, you may be able to point out this need to the school board and other officials.

Ten years ago, sex education was primarily taught to girls in home economics classes. These days, statistics show that the better informed young people are about sex, the more responsible they're likely to be.

Privacy: It's Important!

You know how your parents are always telling you, "Don't just barge into my bedroom. Knock first"? Or, "Go to bed. I need to talk to your dad in private." Parents are entitled to that, for sure. But then again, so are you.

Maybe you've been annoyed lately that Dad comes into your bedroom unannounced. Or that Mom looks at your mail. There's a perfectly good explanation for the way you suddenly value your privacy: You're growing up. You're more aware of your developing body and feel more modest about nudity. You're also establishing your independence—your own world, not Mom's and Dad's—and you like to keep your phone calls and relationships to yourself.

Yet your parents probably aren't quite comfortable with this new you, and sometimes they forget that privacy is your privilege, too. Plus, they worry about you a lot, and think it's necessary to offer advice, help, or restrictions in order to keep you happy and healthy.

How do you balance your own will with those of your parents? Try telling them in a calm, mature way that you *need* your space. "Mom, I know you want to help, but I really want to be alone right now. I would do the same for you, if you asked." Or, "Dad, please don't come into the bathroom when I'm showering. It embarrasses me. If you'll just knock, I'll try to hurry for you."

Obviously, if your home is small, you'll have some limitations. Not all of us have the luxury of our own bedroom. At the same time, you could have a parent who just doesn't understand that you're growing up and deserve your privacy. The only advice we can offer you is keep trying. If you continue to act like an adult, perhaps your parents will learn to respect you as one.

© Leverett Bradley/FPG International

Find private time for yourself. We all need it—at any age.

It's Safe to Be Sexual!

STD's, teenage pregnancy, rape: These are serious subjects, definitely focusing on the down side of sexuality. It's important to know about these things, but it's also important to realize the positive side to sexuality. By making careful decisions and smart moves, you can make growing up anything *but* a negative part of your life. Sexuality is a new and important part of your life, and you're in for a host of new experiences: your first period, first date, first kiss, first boyfriend or girlfriend, and so on. Armed with a solid knowledge of sex and hormonal changes, you can make the transition between childhood and adulthood smoothly, safely, and happily.

GLOSSARY

Abortion The removal of embryonic tissue (belonging to an unborn, undeveloped baby) from the uterus.

Acne A skin condition common to teenagers and young adults. Oil glands become inflamed and cause pimples on the face, chest, and/or back.

Adam's Apple The bump on the front of the neck formed by a part of the larynx.

Amenorrhea An abnormal absence of menstruation.

Anus The opening through which solid wastes pass.

Areolas A ring of skin that surrounds the nipple of the breast. It ranges in color from light pink to brownish black.

Biochemical Having to do with animals (and plants) and their body processes.

Birth Control Devices or actions that prevent pregnancy.

Bisexuality Having to do with sexual relationships between members of either sex, male or female. See also homosexuality, heterosexuality.

Blackhead A black-tipped pimple.

Bladder The body part in which urine is collected.

Breasts The glands on the front chest of a female. They produce milk for her offspring.

Candida Albicans A yeast infection of the vagina caused by the use of certain vaginal products, medications, or hormonal changes. The symptoms include redness, swelling, irritation, and itching of the vulva; a thick, white, cottage-cheese-like discharge; and painful itching.

Cervix In a human female, the passageway between the vagina and uterus.

Circumcision The removal of the foreskin from the penis.

Clitoris Composed of three parts, the glans, the shaft, and the hood, which fill with blood and swell when aroused.

Condom A balloon-shaped sheath of rubber or animal tissue that is placed on the erect penis before sexual activity in order to prevent pregnancy.

Contraceptive A device that prevents pregnancy.

Cyst A closed sac that develops abnormally in or on a part of the body.

Dermatologist A doctor who treats skin and its diseases.

Diaphragm A dome-shaped rubber or plastic device that holds spermicide and is placed into the vagina before sexual intercourse in order to prevent pregnancy.

Douching A way of cleansing the vagina by flushing with a liquid solution.

GLOSSARY

Dysmenorrhea Difficult or painful menstruation.

Ejaculate To discharge semen from the male penis.

Ejaculation The discharge of semen from the male penis.

Engorged To fill with blood or other fluids.

Epididymis A part of the male genitals, located near the testicles.

Epididymitis Inflammation of the epididymis.

Erection The condition in which the male penis fills with blood and becomes rigid.

Estrogen A female hormone made by the ovaries. These hormones bring about sexual changes during puberty: hair around the genitals, menstruation, larger breasts.

Fallopian Tube In a human female, the path which a human egg takes when it travels from ovary to uterus during the menstrual cycle.

Fertilize The unity of a female egg and a male sperm.

Flaccid Limp.

Fluid Retention The condition in which the body does not effectively flush out excess fluids, causing you to feel "bloated."

Foreskin A piece of skin that covers the penis. These days, doctors usually remove the foreskin from babies a few days after birth for hygienic reasons. This is called circumcision.

French Kissing Kissing with an open mouth and using your tongue to touch someone else's mouth.

Gay Having to do with homosexuality—most often among males.

Genitals The reproductive organs.

Gland A cell, tissue, or organ that produces any one of several body fluids, depending on what kind of gland it is. Mammary glands, or breasts, produce milk for babies. The pituitary gland produces a hormone that makes you grow.

Gonads Glands or organs—specifically, the ovaries and testes that produce certain male hormones. These hormones start the changes that transform a child into an adult.

Gynecologist A doctor who treats the diseases and functions of the female.

Heterosexuality Having to do with sexual relationships between members of the opposite sex. See also homosexuality, bisexuality.

Homosexuality Having to do with sexual relationships between members of the same sex. See also heterosexuality, bisexuality.

GLOSSARY

Hormones Body chemicals transported by the blood that bring about change in the body, such as growth and stress.

Hygiene Conditions or habits that promote good health.

Hymen A layer of skin that partially blocks the vaginal opening in young females.

Incest Sexual relationships among family members.

Intrauterine Contraceptive Device (IUD) A mechanical device placed in the uterus to prevent pregnancy.

Learned Behavior An action or response that is not hereditary, but learned. For example, dancing is learned behavior, since you weren't born with the knowledge to dance.

Lesbian A female who is homosexual.

Masturbation A solo sexual act.

Menarche The first menstrual period of a girl.

Menstruation The monthly cycle in a mature female, during which blood and tissues are discharged from the uterus and out of the vagina.

Molest To make hostile sexual advances.

Mucus A thick, slimy secretion that protects and moistens the body's mucous membranes. The nose and vagina have mucous membranes.

Nipple The slightly raised area on the chest, ranging in color from light pink to brownish black. In females, the nipple is the part of the breast through which milk passes for the offspring.

Nocturnal Emission A "wet dream"; when a male ejaculates in his sleep.

Offspring Babies or children.

Orgasm The intense physical and mental reaction—or climax—experienced during a sexual act.

Ova The plural of ovum, a human egg stored in the female.

Ovary Where human eggs are stored in a female.

Ovulation The process by which a female egg matures and escapes from the ovary.

Ovum A human egg, stored in the female.

Pap Test (Papanicolaou's Test) A technique (named for the person who invented it) that tests the female genitals for cancer.

Pedophilia Child molesting.

Pelvic Exam The routine gynecological exam for females.

GLOSSARY

Pelvic Inflammatory Disease (PID) A disorder of the uterus that spreads to the fallopian tubes, ovaries, and surrounding tissues. PID is often introduced into the vagina during sexual intercourse, but it has also been linked to the use of IUD's and abortions. The symptoms include pain during intercourse, pain in the abdomen and back, and a heavy and unpleasant smelling discharge.

Penis The male organ which is inserted into the female's vagina during sexual intercourse. In humans, the penis is also the organ through which urine passes.

Pill, The Medication taken by mouth that prevents pregnancy.

Pimple Any small, rounded, inflamed swelling of the skin. Also called acne.

Pituitary Gland A small, rounded gland in the head that produces certain hormones. These hormones help you grow and help develop your sexual organs.

Pore Tiny openings in the skin through which fluids may be discharged or absorbed.

Pregnancy The condition in which a female carries offspring in her uterus.

Progesterone One of two main female sex hormones (the other is estrogen), which play a part in menstruation and pregnancy.

Prostaglandins Female hormone thought to play a part in menstrual cramps.

Puberty The period of life when a person first becomes able to reproduce sexually.

Pubic Hair Hair that is on or near the genitals of a male or female.

Rape The act of forcing a person to have sex without his or her consent.

Reproduction The process by which animals and plants produce new individuals.

Scrotum The male pouch of skin below the penis that holds the testes.

Sebum The oily secretion produced by glands in the skin.

Secretion A body substance, such as semen or mucus.

Semen The thick, white, creamy fluid that passes out of the penis during ejaculation.

Sexual Intercourse A reproductive act between male and female. In humans, the male inserts his penis into the female's vagina.

Sexually Transmitted Disease (STD) Also called a venereal disease, an STD is an infection passed from person to person through sexual contact.

GLOSSARY

Speculum A medical tool used in gynecological exams, that holds open the vaginal walls.

Sperm The male cell that is passed into the female through sexual intercourse and is capable of fertilizing a female egg.

Spermicide A chemical that kills sperm within the vagina during sexual intercourse in order to prevent pregnancy.

Statutory Rape A legal term describing sexual intercourse between an adult and an underage boy or girl.

Taboo Forbidden by society or tradition. For example, body odor is taboo in most societies of this country.

Testosterone A male hormone produced in the testes.

Testes, Testicles Plural of testis, testicle.

Testis, Testicle In the male, one of two oval sex glands in the scrotum where the hormone testosterone and sperm are made.

Thyroid Gland A gland, located in your neck, that produces certain hormones. These hormones help regulate your growth.

Traits Characteristics or distinguishing features. The trait of a rabbit, for example, is his long ears.

Trichomonas Vaginitis Infection of the vagina that is usually transmitted by sexual intercourse. The symptoms include a heavy, unpleasant smelling and greenish yellow discharge; itching, irritation, swelling, and redness in the vulva.

Urethra The canal through which urine is discharged from the bladder.

Urinary Tract Infection Inflammation of the urethra, the tube that leads from the bladder to the outside. UTI can be passed through sexual intercourse. The symptoms include painful, frequent urination.

Urine The liquid waste product of mammals, usually yellowish and stored in the bladder until discharged.

Uterus The female organ from which menstrual blood originates and in which offspring develop.

Vagina The opening in the female genital area through which menstrual blood passes. This is also where the penis enters during sexual intercourse and where babies pass out at birth.

Vaginitis Any one of several infections of the vagina. The symptoms include redness, swelling, itching, and vaginal discharges.

Vas Deferens In the male, the tubes that carry sperm from the testes to the penis.

GLOSSARY

Virgin A person who has not had sexual intercourse.

Vulva The external genital area of a female.

Whitehead A pimple.

Yeast Infection See candida albicans.

USEFUL ADDRESSES AND ORGANIZATIONS

Alternatives to Abortion International
Eight Cottage Pl.
White Plains, NY 10601

American Social Health Association
260 Sheridan Ave., Suite 307
Palo Alto, CA 94306

American Venereal Disease Association
P.O. Box 22349
San Diego, CA 92122

Carnegie Council on Adolescent Development
c/o Carnegie Corporation of New York
437 Madison Ave.
New York, NY 10022

Citizens Alliance for Venereal Disease Awareness
222 West Adams St.
Chicago, IL 60606

Council for Sex Information and Education
Box 72
Capitola, CA 95010

Foundation for America's Sexually Exploited Children
Route 9, Box 327A
Bakersfield, CA 93312

Herpes Resource Center
P.O. Box 100
Palo Alto, CA 94302

International Council of Sex Education and Parenthood
5010 Wisconsin Ave. N.W.
Washington, D.C. 20016

National Coalition Against Sexual Assault
c/o Volunteers of America
8787 State St., Suite 202
East Saint Louis, IL 62203

National Coalition of Gay Sexually Transmitted Disease Services
P.O. Box 239
Milwaukee, WI 53201

National Family Planning and Reproductive Health Association
122 C St., N.W.
Suite 380
Washington, D.C. 20001

National Organization of Adolescent Pregnancy and Parenting
P.O. Box 2365
Reston, VA 22090

National Youth Pro-Life Coalition
Jackson Ave.
Hastings-on-Hudson, NY 10706

Operation Venus
1213 Clover St.
Philadelphia, PA 19107

People Against Rape
P.O. Box 160
Chicago, IL 60635

Planned Parenthood Federation of America
810 Seventh Ave.
New York, NY 10019

Pro-Choice Defense League
131 Fulton Ave.
Hempstead, NY 11550

Sex Information and Education Council of the United States
80 Fifth Ave., Suite 801
New York, NY 10011

Venereal Disease National Hotline
260 Sheridan Ave.
Palo Alto, CA 94306

Victims Anonymous
9514-9 Reseda Blvd., #607
Northridge, CA 91324

INDEX